THIS BOOK IS FOR YOU IF YOU...

- hold your career back because you fear public speaking

- need to be more visible to build your career and your business

- need to ACE the boardroom but worry you may look a fool if you speak up

- are technically brilliant at your job but not visible (because you keep your head down)

- avoid speaking up in front of large groups

- hate all the eyes on you

- avoid appearing on panels and refuse conference requests

- are senior and need to be seen to be leading from the front

- are a leader and know people expect you to speak at events and town halls

- feel like a lamb to the slaughter in front of large audiences and senior stakeholders

- worry your mind will go blank or you'll blush as soon as you speak under pressure

- would rather stick pins in your eyes than speak in public

- think you're not good enough (other people are naturals)

- think you're not 'intelligent' or 'articulate' enough

- want to appear effortlessly confident in pitches, presentations and boardrooms

- dread the thought of introducing yourself round the table (creeping death)

- think oh **** in the Q&A after a presentation

- hate the thought of being judged

- need confidence to do it, and help **NOW!**

ABOUT THE AUTHOR

Esther Stanhope is an international speaker and personal impact expert from London, UK, known as The Impact Guru.

Coming from a background of live broadcasting at the BBC, she knows how to help people communicate with more confidence and gravitas. Esther's worked with 'Big' personalities, Hollywood stars (Madonna and George Clooney to name but two) and world-class business leaders.

A mum of two, she took a massive leap of faith in 2011 to leave a senior staff role at the BBC to set up her own consultancy business helping professionals to pitch, present and speak with more impact using her finely tuned broadcasting skills.

Esther's previous fear of public speaking, and the thousands of people she's helped since then, led her to write Glossophobia. She shares her unusual secrets to overcome nerves so you can stand in the spotlight and speak confidently in front of audiences of any size.

She's helped clients worldwide including; Barclays, Société Générale, JP Morgan, Deloitte, international lawyers, the UK Government, MOD, African leaders on the Nelson Mandela programme in the USA, as well as major players in the tech, property and creative industries.

From meetings and pitches to conferences and job interviews, Esther helps women and men make a powerful impact and ooze confidence with her practical, fun and easy-to-adopt tips.

EYES AND TOOTH! ESTHER AGE 6 IN 1978

I wasn't always confident

For Adam, Mirabelle and Truman

LET'S CONNECT

If you want more tips, blogs and my fun video tips do go to my website.

You'll love it.

Website: **www.estherstanhope.com**

LinkedIn: **Please connect with me**

Email: **impact@estherstanhope.com**

Twitter: **@EstherStanhope1**

Facebook: **EstherStanhopeImpactGuru**

Published by
Filament Publishing 2019
16, Croydon Road, Waddon,
Croydon, Surrey CR0 4PA,
United Kingdom
Telephone: +44 (0) 20 8688 2598
info@filamentpublishing.com
filamentpublishing.com

Text © Esther Stanhope 2019
Illustrations © LMPP Studio 2019

To find out more about Esther Stanhope,
please visit **estherstanhope.com**

Follow her on twitter at **@EstherStanhope1**
and Instagram at **@estherstanhope**

Cover and book designed by LMPP Studio
lmppstudio.co.uk

Printed by Ashford Colour Press

A CIP catalogue record for this book is
available from the British Library

ISBN 978-1-913192-22-8

Esther Stanhope — Author

"Are you ready to get a massive confidence boost? Read on"

"AARRGGHH!

HOW DO I STOP BLUSHING WHEN I STAND UP IN FRONT OF AN AUDIENCE?"

FOREWORD
VANESSA VALLELY OBE

Author and MD of We Are The City

I first met the power that is Esther Stanhope on the rooftop of Shoreditch House in 2017. I meet lots of wonderful people; however this meeting was on another level. It was like a sun blast of both energy and passion coupled with an extremely humorous outlook on life.

It was clear from the offset that Esther knew her stuff given her background as live producer at the BBC where she got to rub shoulders with Hollywood stars, politicians and business leaders. She told many stories about holding cue cards for the rich and famous, prepping speeches and filling people with the confidence they needed to just go and be magical.

The best bit, she wanted to share what she had learnt about public speaking over the past 27 years with the world.

Music to my ears. We waxed lyrical about the confidence it takes to stand up in front of an audience and to actually believe you know your sh*t!

I completely resonated with everything she had to say and above all the advice and tips she shares at her speaking events and what would be in her forthcoming book!

I SAT THERE WISHING SHE WAS AROUND WHEN I FIRST STARTED MY CAREER.

Years before I began speaking for a living I went through various meltdowns prior to taking any form of stage. On reflection, I passed up far too many opportunities to put myself out there, which was mainly due to my own fear. The over-thinking, the intense prep – and the belief that I had to be an A1 expert to the world and his wife before I could ever speak in public.

The biggest fear being, what if I was asked a question I couldn't answer? What if someone in the audience knew more about the topic than me? What if I had a mind blank? A coughing fit, pronounced a word wrong or even lost my train of thought! My fear was compounded by this image I had in my mind of me standing on a stage with the audience just looking at me silent! There is a way to create that moment, but in a good way!

I am sure Esther will tell you all about it.

WHEN I RECALL MY OWN FEARS AROUND PUBLIC SPEAKING

It wasn't just stages that frightened me, sometimes it was even the confidence to speak up and get my point across in meetings. I feared all of the above issues plus a few more to boot. What if my idea got shot down? I'd probably raise my voice again. Things did get easier, it comes with practice, feeling the fear and doing it anyway, plus a good book packed full of useful tips, eg this one!

I absolutely recommend this book as an aid for my own audience at WeAreTheCity and the hundreds of individuals I speak to on a regular basis. At some point in our careers we will all have to address an audience of some sort. It is important that we don't fear these occasions, and that we embrace and enjoy them!

This book is packed to the brim with real life tips from someone who spent her life behind the camera coaching others to be at their absolute best. Whether you are in the corporate, public or creative side of the world, this book will guide you and advise you so you can smash that presentation and feel comfortable on any stage, at any time.

Please don't let opportunities pass you by! Get up, share your voice and be heard. Esther is going to show you how!

ENJOY!

CHAPTER 1

HOW TO SP

GLOSSOPHO

OT

BIA

Cold sweat dripped down my back and my mind went completely blank as I stepped up to the podium at the world-famous Edinburgh International Television Festival, the UK's prestigious global event of the year!

The two steps up onto the stage should have been easy, but I was wearing a slightly tight skirt, so I had to lift it awkwardly to give my legs enough room to climb the stairs.

Oops, fail.

I started my presentation and I had an out-of-body experience! I remember looking down on myself thinking: "What are you saying? You're talking nonsense."

This was early in my broadcasting career before I started my own business and before my BBC producer days – and before I even knew what Glossophobia was.

I thought, like 75% of the world's population, I had a healthy fear of public speaking. But this was something else. This was a physical reaction I'd never felt before. All I could think at the time was –

"I hate this sensation of all eyes on me, I want to curl up in a hole and die!"

Turns out, I wasn't alone. I have met and helped thousands of people who have suffered from Glossophobia. Have you ever felt like that?

When I gave my crappy speech that day, I was Head of Programmes for a 'Yoof' TV Channel called Rapture TV. This was the 'revolutionary' new 'multi-platform' channel aimed at young people. The festival audience of highly successful senior TV execs, commissioners and producers was desperate to hear how to attract the most difficult of TV audiences – 'young people,' – the 16-24 year old market. I was the EXPERT they had come to see, pressure. My session was seriously packed out, it was standing room only, pressure. They wanted to know how we had created this amazing NEW "live clubbing experience". Pressure. So the expectations were H....h....h...high! (I'm getting goose bumps at the very thought of my anxiety that day.)

On that day, the nerves choked me. I played a few of the pre-recorded videos (phew) which luckily helped buffer the fact I was a nervous presenter.

My message got lost in my sea of anxiety. I fumbled over words and didn't get to the point, skipped slides, jumbled words around, stuttered and did a lot of umm, errr, umming!

I did everything on the *'How Not To Approach Public Speaking'* list! Arrhh, I am embarrassed to say I sucked!

My colleagues were shocked. Even though I am an extrovert and people think I am REALLY confident, what they didn't know – and what I discovered to my horror that day – was that I wasn't confident enough on the inside to stand in front of a crowd of people and share my message under pressure.

I SUFFERED FROM GLOSSOPHOBIA! THE FEAR OF PUBLIC SPEAKING.

DA DA DAAAAAAA.

APPARENTLY 75% OF US
SUFFER FROM THIS TYPE
OF ANXIETY — WHICH HAS
DEVASTATING SIDE EFFECTS.

DO THESE
SYMPTOMS SOUND FAMILIAR?

- *Pounding heart rate (you can hear it beating in your head)*

- *Blood pressure going up, up, up*

- *A red rash*

- *Sweaty palms, sweaty everything*

- *Quick, shallow, 'goldfish' breaths*

- *Upset stomach/nauseous*

- *Feeling light-headed and fuzzy*

- *Stiff neck and upper back muscles*

- *Shaking hands*

- *Quivering voice*

- *Dry-as-paper mouth*

- *A hamster wheel of negative thoughts running obsessively in your head.*

It was a bloody horror show.

I also didn't realise until 5 years ago (nearly 20 years later) that my Glossophobia had been one of the main reasons I had held myself back in my career.

HAVE YOU EVER FELT LIKE THIS?

DOES GLOS

HOLD YOU

OPHOBIA
BACK?

Many of my clients in business have described similar side effects, as well as shaking, coming out in a rash, having to take Diazepam (yes, I'll talk about this later in the book) and total brain freeze!

There's good news!

Since then, I have learnt how to be comfortable in front of audiences of every size and to make an impact on them. Yes. I have transformed by learning from others and understanding that everyone is different. I have learnt to trust myself and that venturing outside your comfort zone is a good thing. I have learnt that failure is sometimes the fastest way to improve and grow in confidence.

Since my shaky day in Scotland all those years ago, I have helped thousands of speakers all over the world including BBC presenters, politicians and business leaders from global organisations (banks, law firms and FTSE 100 firms), nail their speeches despite their Glossophobia - fear of public speaking.

I have also mastered the art of speaking to a large audience myself! (And finding joy in it.)

Can you believe standing on a stage in front of hundreds of people has become my comfort zone? It could be yours!

But first, I'd be happy to see you feeling comfortable standing up and speaking up in a meeting of three people.

JUST AS I HAD TO DO.

The shaky, red-faced, stumbling Esther has changed. And there's one thing I know for sure; if I can master it, you can. You'll transform your confidence and your business when you learn to speak up in meetings, pitches, in the boardroom and even in front of a larger audience – like at a town hall or a conference, on a panel or even on TV.

I was inspired to write this book because I have spoken to thousands of people, close friends, colleagues and clients, who have suffered just like me. And the transformation when they've tackled their demons and faced glossophobia head on (with my help) is extraordinary. At the BBC I was a behind-the-scenes person. As a senior producer I launched TV Presenter Vanessa Feltz's radio show and looked after the likes of Boris Johnson and Theresa May live on air. I was the one shouting from behind the glass "go on, you're brilliant darling, eyes and teeth, roll VT!"

But I didn't have the confidence to be in front of the camera or audiences. I've learnt first-hand (and so have hundreds of my clients) that the power of public speaking is essential to build a successful career and do better business.

"Esther has been a game changer for me personally and for my status in the market, which has led to more business for the bank. Esther is brilliant and fun to work with. I would not hesitate in recommending her, particularly to senior women who often avoid the spotlight"

Senior leader, Barclays Bank

You can attract more clients after learning the art of confident speaking. I've seen senior leaders get promoted because they learnt to manage their 'Panel-nerves'. Many of my clients have made multi-million-dollar deals because they've mastered the art of getting their voices heard loud and clear in Exec committee meetings.

There's NO downside to combatting Glossophobia.

It changes your life, your inner confidence and your career!

You can do it too. You can learn to combat those speaking nerves. Are you ready?

Read on...

NOTE TO WOMEN

There's one other alarming thing I've discovered!

I've travelled the world helping business professionals from all over (particularly women in business). My observation? Women are much less likely than men to stand up and put themselves in the spotlight. There. I've said it. I thought it was just me. Hey, men struggle with Glossophobia too, but in business how many women compared to men do you see speaking at conferences, podiums, or the town hall standing in front of large audiences – in the spotlight? This is another reason I decided to write this pocket guide for you.

This is a call to action for women!

It's quick, easy to follow, fun and full of practical tips that demystify the art of speaking up in front of people – in the board room, in the meeting, in the presentation or at the conference. It's your time to be visible, and to be a role model. It's your time to speak up in meetings, on panels and get yourself behind podiums and on stages. Whatever and wherever you'd like.

And to always feel like yourself.

Are you ready to take a deep breath and start your journey into the spotlight?

Ready for the Esther Stanhope Experience? Brace yourself.

Keily Blair, Lawyer

CHAPTER 2
HOW DO I START?

STOP!

That's how you start. Don't even THINK about writing a script for your meeting or presentation.

Put the pen **DOWN!**

Don't worry, I know you're obsessed with the excruciating blank sheet of paper and this is probably whirring around your head...

*"I don't know what I'm going to say, I need to prepaaaaaare, I need to get the script written, I need to research **EVERYTHING** I could possibly be asked about XYZ, I need to get my junior to get ALL the slides from XYZ, the facts, figures, graphs, visuals, yes, some photographs to liven it up, yes the old deck will have lots of useful information I can use...*

*...I need to **KNOW EVERYTHING**, then I will know what I have to say and I'll be an expert. I'll be confident when I KNOW everything and I'm prepared with a script that's right and correct with CLEVER things in it that make me look credible and CLEVER and confident...etc...etc..."*

You don't need to re-invent the wheel and know EVERYTHING about EVERYTHING... you don't even need to do half the work you think you need to do.

Recently, one of my very senior clients, let's call him 'Matt', was about to give the presentation of his life at the global partners' conference in a large hotel in London to around 700 lawyers worldwide.

He wanted his speech to be BRILLIANT, he wanted to KNOW EVERYTHING, he wanted to have super-clever visuals, images and a beautifully crafted deck that people would go 'WOW' to.

He invested a lot of time and money to have me as his personal one–to–one speaking expert, so I was delighted to help.

He was so obsessed (in a good way, he was very passionate and wanted to do well) with this being the most excellent performance of his life that he did almost every single thing you SHOULDN'T do when starting the process of public speaking.

He did all the usual things you think you should do when you are under extreme pressure and don't want to 'get it wrong'.

When he revealed to me the importance of his mission – to nail this career-changing presentation – I realised he'd already started (without me).

He hadn't brought me in at 'The Blank Sheet' stage. I must say, I started to get a bit hot under the collar as we sat on a Sunday afternoon around the pristine boardroom table on the 8th floor of the deserted law firm in London. I knew he had already wasted a ton of time and money. He had already commissioned a very expensive design agency to 'pimp up his slides'.

He had colours, he had words (oh yes, lots of words), he had animated graphs that would grow and move as he went through the slides one by one.

Now, I'm not usually for lost for words. But the sheer size of his 'deck' totally freaked me out. He whacked this vast pile of paper onto the shiny wooden table, BANG!

There was a silence and he looked at me…

"Do you think there are too many slides" he asked.

"Um, how many slides do you have there?"

He had 199 slides! He looked at me with his eyebrows in the air and this made me laugh…

"Do you think there are too many?" he asked again.

It was hilarious. The only answer to that question was this BIG tip. I asked him…

"What does your AUDIENCE need?"

I call this little exercise the 'Audience Audit' – I asked him…

"If you were sitting in the auditorium expecting a 40-minute ground-breaking speech and I revealed I had 199 slides to share with you. How would you feel?"

"I'd probably want to kill you!" he said.

Hallelujah! I suggested we put the 'deck' to one side for a minute and start with: A Blank Sheet.

So that's what we did. And that's what you're going to do too.

How do you start – you STOP!

(More on this in chapter 8)

**Don't present what you want to say –
present what your audience needs to hear.**

**(The only reason to give a presentation is to affect an
audience. The presentation is for their benefit, not
yours, and if your message is right for them,
they'll love you!)**

**Lee Warren, author of
'The Busy Person's Guide To Great Presenting'**

CHAPTER 3
WHAT IF I FAIL?

You won't fail if you read this book – or pick out the parts that are helpful to you.

Here's why you're not going to fail.

I have tried and tested all the tips in this pocket guide and I have heard hundreds of stories from clients all over the world, in banks, law firms and global organisations and at my time at the BBC.

One of the main reasons for Glossophobia – fear of public-speaking is because you may have failed to speak with confidence at some point in the past.

EYES AND TOOTH!
ESTHER AGE 6 IN 1978
– I wasn't always confident

For me, if I trace my Glossophobia back, it all started when I was six. My teacher at Little Ealing School in West London, Miss Baldock (I hated her), asked me to read aloud to the class of 33 children. I failed. All the words on the page seemed to disintegrate and I couldn't get the words out. I was tongue-tied. I started to sweat and shake, I couldn't speak properly and so I was labelled dumb.

That was why I believe I failed again at the Edinburgh TV festival 20 years later. A bad experience in the past doesn't mean you can't achieve confident speaking NOW!

The most common reasons for failure:

1. Bad experience in past, for example a school play, or a music exam

2. You stepped in for someone else and used their material – you failed to 'own' it.

3. Someone senior told you what to say and how to say it – aarrgghh fatal

4. You thought you had to be 'like them' – you compared yourself to someone you thought was brilliant at speaking, therefore you told yourself you were rubbish!

5. You tried to deliver the 'information' you thought you needed to deliver but failed in the execution (maybe it felt like an execution- aarrgghh.)

QUICK STORY ABOUT FAILURE...

Betty, a very good friend and client of mine, had to deliver a new way of working to her organisation. She worked in a well-respected global bank and they were bringing in a new coaching programme to help senior leaders.

She was asked to present their 'new way forward' to around 500 people at one of their town hall events in Europe. Her boss had been integral to the presentation content. He had told her what to say and what to put on the slides. Can you already spot the big mistake? She wasn't owning it from the beginning.

As a result she had lots of slides, data, graphs, a detailed analysis of the new coaching model, lots of script to learn and a whole heap of anxiety.

This type of prep feeds Glossophobia and, I'm afraid, puts you on the path to certain failure...

AARRGGHH! SOUND FAMILIAR?

Have you ever had to do a presentation that someone else has 'told' you to do? Hmmm don't worry, you won't have to again. So Betty, being a good girl, learnt all her lines – pages and pages of script.

She practised and practised and practised, she ran the lines, she had the perfect 'deck' and she wore smart clothes. All very important. She did everything that was technically required of her that day.

BUT... she failed to do the one thing she needed to succeed in public speaking. She failed to think about her audience and, therefore, failed to win them over. She didn't get people gushing, **_"You were wonderful darling"_** afterwards. Instead, she got silence. Halfway through she started losing it; she realised she was looking into a sea of blank faces.

This was her moment of Glossophobia, the fear of public speaking. She wasn't being herself, she wasn't owning it, and she forgot her lines because she was totally freaked out.

But the good news is, this failure taught her a lesson. It taught her to find HER own way, to be herself, to go with her gut when it comes to thinking about her audience.

Her failure became the biggest learning curve of her life. Now Betty has moved on in her career and has successfully moved on with her public speaking achievements.

She is comfortable in her own skin, and comfortable in front of an audience.

In short, **SHE OWNS IT**. So can you.

What if you fail? If you do, remember what they do in Silicone Valley – fail fast, learn and move on! Then it's not a fail, it's a school of life.

CHAPTER 4
BE YOU—ISH

"Be yourself;
everyone else
is already
taken."

Oscar Wilde

The first step in facing Glossophobia is to understand yourself. And then be yourself.

Here's a contrarian thought for you.

The more you can be yourself at work, the better. Yes, really, warts and all. You need to be YOU-ISH.

KAREN—ISH!!

Being you-ish is really being unafraid to be yourself –

just as the Oscar Wilde quote:

"Be yourself; everyone else is already taken"

It's YOU at the bar, YOU chatting confidently with your pals about something you feel passionate about, YOU when you are doing something you love...do you laugh?

What makes YOU, YOU?

I often explain to clients, we want more YOU at the bar in the boardroom please.

(OK, without the swear words)

**I describe this confident,
fun YOU as:**

YOU—ISH.

Do you have a strong
'personal brand'?

If you do, people remember you and
you'll do better business!

It does require you to use your quirks
and oddities though.

Do you use yours?

TANTALISING TIP

Remember that the audience is on your side.

(They aren't the enemy waiting for you to fail – they actually want you to succeed so you can all have a good time.)

I always channel the energy I got when I did my wedding speech and there was 'so much love in the room' for me and my husband! Remembering those warm, smiling faces always gives me a big boost.

Kim Arnold
Business Growth Consultant
& Communication Coach

CHAPTER 5
MAKE YOUR ODDITY
YOUR ASSET!

Confession. I'M ODD

I've been called a fruitcake, a box of frogs, bonkers, eccentric, quirky, weird, lunatic and slightly mad... in a good way.

Ok, one of my oddities is the fact I can remember your clothes! Yes, whatever you wore last time we met (whatever year), I can probably remember the patterned shirt, the blue tie, the black & white dress or the statement bling-necklace (that's easy).

When my mum talks about being a teacher in the 1970s, I can remember the outfits.

"Oh yes, you wore the purple blouse with small white buttons and dangly earrings on my 5th birthday" – weird.

The other day my whole family stayed over at a friend's house in Henley near Oxford and we got talking about this odd phenomenon.

"So what were we wearing yesterday?" they were testing me.

"Well you'd been running and she was wearing a turquoise top which matched Tom's stripes down his black shorts" – that's just **OOOODDDDD!**

I've realised my 'odd' talent illustrates the way my brain works – yes, it's strange but I have a super-photographic memory for selective things. I also love to observe people.

Hey, that's what I've been doing for years in my career in broadcasting and business – observing people and painting a picture of them in my mind. It's a useful tool to remember small details about people – this has helped me build relationships quickly – a fantastic business skill and a huge asset.

Ha ha I'm not alone – I bet you have your weird quirks too. I know you have.

What's your oddity? Do you celebrate it?

The other day I was with clients in London and we started to share our odd stuff while we sat round the table in my session. We chatted about the weird things you don't think are important, but which are just part of you.

We couldn't stop laughing. One amazing woman, the leader in her team of highly experienced insurance professionals, was forced to come out (as it were) about her tendency to...

"COLLECT BUTTERS"

Yes, Xina collects little portions of butter and other stuff "like a squirrel" she explained, "just in case people need it at lunchtime."

"She's odd, quite eccentric," they went on, "she'll try anything".

This petite and feisty leader has tea-danced in a room filled with 100 Chinese grandparents, she's tried flower arranging and skydiving. She likes to keep life interesting. What a woman; don't you love her already?

That's a pretty good character trait. Her stories show she is curious and open to new ideas.

HER ODD IS HER ASSET. AS IT IS FOR YOU.

TALENTED TIP

The traditional view is that, to have gravitas, you need a deep voice. That's not true.

But what does undermine your gravitas is when your voice goes up at the end of your sentences, making everything you say sound like a question. Try making your voice go down at the end instead. And add a pause to let the point land.

Antoinette Dale Henderson, Gravitas Expert, Speaker and Executive Coach

Do you have a strange habit, a skill or a musical talent that you can turn into an asset?

I bet you have.

Your quirks are also your strengths.

PRACTICAL TIP

Write down your weird quirks and see if you can find a pattern, something that makes you who you are. What do people say about you? Think of something you find easy but others don't.

Make a list of your oddities and examples.

It's important to find your 'ODD-ness' and embrace it. It's your USP. Your USP is your "Unique Selling Point" or as my Canadian client said the other day in one of my masterclasses, "your unique selling proposition".

What's the one thing people say about you when you leave the room?

What's your quirk? You know...how people might describe you.

Do they say, "You know the bright little spark", "The tall German compliance woman" or "You know, she's the head of HR with a smile which means – she's alright, she's one of us!"

No one wants a 'cookie cutter'. They don't want you to be the same as anyone else. You bring your own uniqueness into the room. You fill it with YOU-ish ness!

HERE'S WHY ODD IS GOOD...

PEOPLE CAN SEE YOU'RE BEING REAL.
IT SHOWS YOUR PERSONAL SIDE.
IT HELPS THEM TO CONNECT WITH
YOU FASTER. COPYING SOMEONE ELSE
NEVER WORKS.

I AM A FAN
OF BEING GOOFY

Seriously, yes, I mean I am very professional. Haven't you noticed?

And I'm telling you with a totally straight face, look, no smirking, stop it now

.... BE GOOFY!

Let me tell you why.

A fiercely bright and creative account manager from one of the biggest advertising agencies in the world had a session with me.

Let's call her 'Coco'. Here's Coco's story.

Can you relate to it?

COCO FELT...

– She was being overlooked for promotions because she wasn't one of the 'loud ones' in meetings.

– Desperately unconfident in formal meetings with senior people.

– Terrified of public speaking – she had Glossophobia big time!

– The more 'professional' and 'perfect' she tried to be, the less she spoke up.

– That, behind the scenes she was brilliant at her job.

– She was brilliant at dealing with the tricky 'creatives' and 'difficult' people.

- At home with her family she was outgoing and fun, yet at work she was stifled.

- **INVISIBLE.**

When we had our session and I asked her about being herself at work, she

looked at me and said...

"BUT I CAN'T BE MYSELF, THAT WOULD BE UNPROFESSIONAL"

Have you ever felt like that?

I was shocked, although this is a common belief, particularly in well-known and well-respected global organisations.

I was shocked, because in a creative organisation you'd think people would feel 'free' to be themselves. You'd think a creative agency would push the 'be yourself' message because you need people to have a voice and come up with fresh ideas on a daily basis. If you feel stifled, you won't be able to be creative and try new things; you'll be too scared.

In a bank or law firm I can understand why people think they "need to be very professional" so they fear "being themselves".

One of my clients, Harry from East London, told me,

"I can't be myself like I am with my mates down the pub because that would come across as unprofessional at the bank."

I suggested that he try it, but omit the swear words! He laughed and agreed to give it a go. He reported back a week later with an email that read…

"You're right, I had a much better client meeting and I was actually funny in the Monday conference call. People actually listened for once."

I thought of Harry and asked Coco how her friends and family would describe her if they were having a drink at the pub (that's a good indicator of how much you're truly being yourself at work). She blushed and proceeded to tell me about her 'goofiness', how she always sees the funny side to life and pipes up with ridiculous comments and gets into silly situations.

I told her.

"If you have a sense of humour and you're a bit goofy – then BE GOOFY, be odd, burst into song if you have to."

"But will I look unprofessional?" you ask.

The trick is for your humour to be what I call
AAH – Audience-Appropriate Humour!

You have to manage your goofiness wisely. Coco did use her goofiness wisely after our one–to–one sessions. And here's what she wrote to me two weeks later…

"Thank you SO much, I have noticed a massive boost in my confidence. I am already believing more in my own value which is surprising and great! I'm being goofier."

Since writing this, Coco has started to celebrate her inner goofiness and is more confident, happier and on her path to career success. Hurray!

You can't please everyone all of the time. However, when there's a good fit with your audience, they will love the goofy and human side of you. And this helps them to remember you and your message.

Remember

AAH

Audience   Appropriate   Humour!

BE YOURSELF — GET ON YOUR PATH AND DON'T WORRY ABOUT WHAT PEOPLE THINK OF YOU

When it comes to public speaking, your audience will appreciate your humour and you for being you.

TERRIFIC TIPS

– Use the power of three – people remember things in threes!

– Keep slides to a minimum and don't overcrowd them. Use that white space.

– Be engaging and smile.

– Be human.

– Be brief.

– Don't overstay your welcome, leave them wanting more.

– Practise, practise, practise & when you get fed up of that practise some more.

– Only tell a joke if you're good at telling jokes – otherwise leave it to the professionals.

– Know your subject, don't bluff, you'll get found out.

– Don't forget to breathe!

Stephen Murtagh MBA, Entertainment Industry, UK

CHAPTER 6
CELEBRATE YOUR HASHTAG

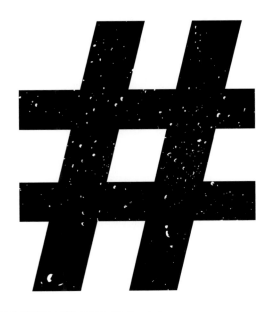

WHAT'S YOUR HASHTAG

First of all, you might be asking: **'What is a hashtag Esther?'**

Some clients ask me this as they aren't too familiar with social media. A hashtag is a word or phrase used on social media platforms like Twitter, Facebook or Instagram to describe a topic in an irreverent way. For example: **#HappyFriday, #PowerfulWomen** or **#Glossophobia.**

This exercise is not necessarily for social media – it's for YOU. It's a short cut to knowing who you are in a few short words. It's your quick fix to discover your personal brand.

Try this fun hashtag game with colleagues, clients and friends. It's a fantastic way to talk about yourself without feeling self-conscious and it always gets people laughing and coming up with crazy ideas. A brilliant ice-breaker to use on a staff awayday!

ASK YOURSELF THIS.
IF YOU HAD A HASHTAG
WHAT WOULD IT BE?

Make up a hashtag for yourself that describes YOU in the shortest way possible.

Don't worry, you don't have to be super creative and over-think your hashtag, and you don't have to get it tattooed onto your left buttock either!

The handy thing about this exercise is that when you know your hashtag, you know how to be YOU-ish.

The best hashtags have a cultural reference and a hint of your personality that's totally unique to you.

One head of finance created the hashtag for herself...

#Fun_Finance_Head

"Ahh", I said, *"that's an oxymoron"* (when you describe things with two opposites) Another oxymoron hashtag I came across in a French bank was ...

#Happy_Parisienne

Apparently Parisiennes aren't known for being 'happy'.

My favourite #hashtag belongs to my client who says she is the only person in compliance who has an 'outgoing' personality. She's done one of those popular psychometric tests based on colours – have you ever done one?

Her hashtag is:

#The_Only_Yellow_In_Compliance

Very funny; it made me laugh!

If your hashtag helps you stand out from the crowd, that's a good thing. Have a go and bring your background, culture or hobby into it. If you're Italian, make your hashtag Italian, if you're from Essex, celebrate it.

We've had a **#Brainy_Bronx_Girl** before.

Go on – this hashtag WILL help you figure out your authentic voice. Live by your hashtag and share it with your nearest and dearest.

Once you've decided what your hashtag is, you can channel it when you speak in a meeting, on a conference call, or on stage at a conference. It's your essence, it's what people will know you for.

Use it, celebrate it, enjoy it.

And what am I famous for?

#EyesAndTeeth

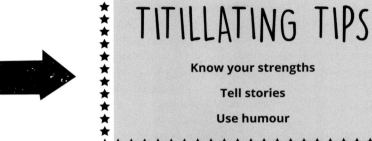

TITILLATING TIPS

Know your strengths

Tell stories

Use humour

I focus on bringing things to life, explaining using everyday language with real life examples. This engages the audience because I am comfortable, and raises smiles and occasional laughs without effort!

CHAPTER 7 —
MAKE THE AUDIENCE
FALL IN LOVE WITH YOU

Here's the brutal truth. It's a shocker.

Your audience only takes in a teeny tiny chunk of your presentation. They may only take away one thing. Most of that isn't what you actually say.

They only remember WHAT THEY FEEL.

So when you make it short, sweet and entertaining, you are more likely to make a positive impact and impression.

You probably think what I used to think...

"Oh no, what am I going to say? I need to be clever, I need to come across as credible, I need to know everything in case they ask me something, I need to know more than the audience, I need to be perfect, I CAN'T make a fool of myself, I need, I need, I need etc."

You don't need all these things. You certainly don't need to be a professor to craft killer content; you don't need to show people you are 'clever'. In fact you don't even need to spend LOADS of time crafting your content.

Good news. You can craft great content with much less effort than you think.

OK, I know I'm from the BBC and the Beeb became famous for 'dumbing things down'.

But this isn't about dumbing things down – this is about not boring the pants off people!

Does your audience really want you to be intellectual? Really?

Are you doing a lecture at Oxford? Even then, does the audience want you to dazzle them with intellectual superiority?

What they want is to hear the energy and fire in your message. And why they should care about it.

My lovely client Amy – a managing partner at a global firm – had to do a "public address" to her 800–strong audience of professionals.

She was **"TERRIFIED!"** In fact, she used to avoid public speaking at all costs before she met me.

When we had our first session she was obsessing about the cynics, the people who hadn't bought into her **'new regime'.** She thought people might hate her and she was afraid of standing on the podium with the pressure that she wasn't liked.

She was self-conscious and felt she didn't have the right background or intellect compared to the some of the **'clever, Oxbridge-Educated'** cynics.

Amy wanted to craft a 'clever' intellectually rich speech to make herself feel better. She thought her speech had to be filled with clever facts, figures and witty comments, just like "the posh blokes in the audience". She thought she had to out-wit them.

Imagine the pressure of trying to outwit the cynics as well as the pressure of having Glossophobia. She needed some serious reassurance. Also, I knew she had the potential to be brilliant.

I told her...

"NOOOOOO!"

It wasn't the right approach at all. She had to be herself and in the words of my daughter, "keep it real".

My advice to her and to you...

Forget about the cynics, forget about trying to be 'clever'. Forget about trying to outwit your colleagues.

Concentrate on engaging with the bulk of the audience. Guess what? They aren't out to get you. They want to learn from you. They want you to succeed. They don't care THAT much.

THE WAY YOU MAKE YOUR AUDIENCE FALL IN LOVE WITH YOU IS BY DOING A BRILLIANT BRAIN—DUMP—AUDIENCE—AUDIT BEFORE YOU CREATE YOUR PRESENTATION. I HAD AMY GET SOME BLANK PAPER.

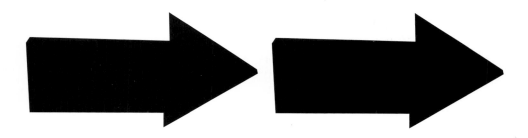

The first thing we did was understand what the audience actually needed. Turns out what they really wanted was to get to know Amy as a person, her background, her health issues (she had a rare condition but hadn't talked about it publicly). They also wanted to know if she was going to make any major changes to the firm that would affect their lifestyle, pay, and job prospects!

This isn't intellectual stuff; it requires a simple audience-audit-brain-dump on paper! Jot down everything you might want to put into your speech that you think the audience will **LOVE** – the stories, facts, problem-solving, innovation, plans and vision.

Notice – you are brain-dumping what the audience will **LOVE** versus what you **THINK** you **SHOULD** put into a clever speech! Turns out the content you write down on the audience-brain-dump is very different from the slide deck you thought you **SHOULD** work from.

 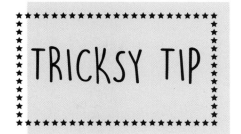

TRICKSY TIP

Remember, no one in the room knows the subject matter better than you.

Having confidence that I know my subject inside out takes away some of the nerves because, even if I forget "my lines", then I am certain I know enough about the subject matter and can focus my attention on staying calm, breathing, talking slowly and giving a coherent and engaging talk.

Sarah Kerrigan, Executive Assistant and Author of 'The Travel Secret: How to plan your big trip and see the world'

CHAPTER 8
THE MAGIC STARTS WITH CREATIVE CHUNKS

A very good friend of mine, Nicki, a highly successful business tycoon who LOVES speaking in front of audiences, told me a great tip when it comes to content...

"Chunk it up"

Quite simply – gather up chunks of content:

– Stories – I remember the day my boss called me at 11pm and revealed...

– Observations – have you noticed women tend to not speak up in meetings?

– Stats – did you know 99% of people do this?

– Quotes – Be yourself; everyone else is already taken – Oscar Wilde

– Tips – breathe slowly for 45 seconds to get rid of cortisol (the stress hormone)

TERRIFYINGLY TRUTHFUL TIP

Imagine you are trying to explain things to a group of friends or friendly colleagues.

In my case it is intellectual vanity too. I changed careers. I was Of Counsel at another firm but wanted a different work-life balance. I am now "just" a professional support lawyer, and when I speak externally now it's usually because of my academic articles. I positively enjoy the return to the limelight... and the surprise in people's faces that I actually know what I am talking about.

You take exceeding expectations to another level.

Anon – Lawyer

CHAPTER 9
HOW TO CREATE A DELICIOUS BITE—SIZED CONTENT CHUNK

TRÉS BON TIP

**Just say yes
(even if you really don't like public speaking).**

Sue McLean – Partner at a global law firm

A QUICK AND EASY FOUR—STEP GUIDE TO CREATING YOUR PERFECT ELEVATOR PITCH

This is my client Sasha's four step elevator pitch about her £10 million success story.

STEP 1: HAVE A HEADLINE.

"Would you like to know how we grew Client X from £100,000 to £10 million in under four years?"

STEP 2: SHARE A STORY.

Paint a beautiful picture to illustrate your headline. Now we're getting into being more you-ish! *"10 million dollars all started with a scarf."*

"My client Lara was the senior decision maker. Before one strategy meeting, she commented on my red scarf and we got talking about how much we hate shopping. We just hit it off, and since then we've been for a few long lunches where we've discussed scarves, accessories and the project. We realised that there was a lot more we could do and four years later we've grown the project and multiplied into other workstreams and they are now a £10 million client."

Hey, if you're thinking "I don't have a £10 million project" story, don't worry, this is a one-off. It's the perfect example of someone who used to undersell herself. It's a story about how she built her relationship from a very small thing. The shopping trip and lunches painted a picture to illustrate it with colour and freshness.

STEP 3: ADD A FEELING. FEELINGS ARE FAR MORE INTERESTING THAN FACTS!

Put yourself in the hot seat. Ask yourself this question: "How do I feel about it?" If you work in the City you won't get asked the question, "How do you feel about it?" It's the sort of question a journalist would ask you because you're more likely to get a more 'touchy feely' answer – something that comes from the heart – rather than the spreadsheet!

In the Impact Guru school of Glossophobia (all those years at the BBC have rubbed off) I've learnt that, when you share how you feel, you're using emotional words that help you connect with your audience quickly. Putting a feeling into your story makes it yours, it makes it authentic, it makes it 'real' – rather than the answer you could have cut and pasted from any website.

What did Sasha ask herself? And then SHARE in her speech?

"I am delighted to have Lara as a client, we just get on, she makes me laugh and we have a giggle about things. It makes it so much easier to do business when you know someone like that and have a close relationship."

That is not the 'corporate zombie' answer.

STEP 4: WHAT DOES IT MEAN FOR THE FUTURE?

This wraps it up in a nutshell super-fast. It finishes off with a What Next? Or even an action. In Sasha's case...

"We already have plans for the next three years and we'll continue to work closely on this. We can also roll out some of our project ideas to other clients because we are finessing them with Client X."

Always finish on a high! Looking into the future helps you come across like a leader.

Have a go at answering any question using the formula.

– Top line – or a killer headline

– Example – tell a story to back it up

– Feeling – how do you feel about it?

– What does it mean for the future?

Get cracking.

Create content chunks. This will help you be more efficient with your prep and transform the way you feel about presenting forever!

Brainstorm and write down ideas for chunks of content you could use for presentations, pitches or speeches. Don't filter YET, just start gathering useful stuff that may or may not be used in your next speaking engagement.

CHAPTER 10
THE 0—10 SECOND RULE

"It takes me a few minutes to get into the swing of it, then I'm OK," says my client (let's call her Toni) about her board meetings and presentations.

"I'm pretty shaky at the beginning and my voice goes a bit, then after I've done the intro, about three minutes in, I'm fine. My hands stop shaking, my voice stops quivering and I can relax into it, and even enjoy it."

I was with my client other day and she shared this with me, looking rather pleased with herself. She's a senior partner at a top global law firm and she's been practicing law and speaking to audiences for 25 years.

Sound familiar?

"Hmmm," I say *"yes, most of us take a while to warm up, which is why you need to do the warming up AWAY from the audience – before you speak!"*

I call it the GOLDEN HOOK. (More on this technique in the next chapter!)

Toni was interested. I shared this advice with her and you too can learn from this tip, so you don't make the same very common mistake again.

I've got good news and bad news... are you ready?

THE GOOD NEWS? IT'S NOT AS DIFFICULT AS YOU THINK.

You will get good at this.

You can relax and enjoy your presentations
and high-pressure meetings in the future and yes,
you can seriously nail your next one.

THE BAD NEWS — YOU LOST YOUR AUDIENCE LAST TIME!

Here's the truth:

– After the first ten seconds, unless you gave them a hook, the audience didn't hear a message and started to disengage.

– After 30 seconds if you were still shaky, all they were thinking was, "oh no, he's a bit nervous, poor guy, I know how he feels."

– After one minute they were thinking, "I wonder how long this is going to go on for?"

By minute three Toni didn't realise that, even though SHE felt confident, her fabulous content was falling on deaf ears because...

The audience wasn't engaged!

Her mistake:

- She didn't hit the ground running with a big Whoosh!
- She didn't warm up her vocal chords and body so she was physically firing on all cylinders (this is what I've learned from producing talent at the BBC and it works!).
- She didn't give the audience what they NEEDED in the first 0-10 seconds.

More good news...

Your content is all there – the overall delivery is great – and it's really easy to polish up your act and make the most of what you've got (and you've got it, I know you have). Make sure your opener is on fire – there are some cool killer opener ideas in the next chapter!

Don't you make the same mistake as Toni and throw your ten-second golden hook time down the loo.

CHAPTER II
THE GOLDEN HOOK

The YouTube generation has an attention span of around three seconds!

As we've established the 0 - 10 second rule – here's HOW you can quickly create your golden hook or TOP LINE to grab the audience's attention.

You know, something that will make them sit up and take note.

At the BBC we used to call it a 'prick up your ears moment' in the live radio show.

Your hook time, (I like to call this 'Golden Hook Time), is that 0-10 second zone. All audiences need this – whether it's an audience of 1, your boss, 1,000 staff at the town hall or half a million on a radio show – the killer top line is essential.

A very good friend of mine, Celia Delaney, a fellow speaker, (award winning) cabaret artist and comedienne, summed up a good opener with these three suggestions to grab your audience hook, line and sinker...

STORY

STATEMENT

QUESTION

The trick is to target your audience and give them something that will be 100% relevant at that moment. It's called The Golden Hook!

So for example if you're talking to an audience of senior women lawyers who want to get promoted – create your opener like this...

1 — STORY

Start with a story. It could be about a sassy senior lawyer called Elise who missed out on a career opportunity because she didn't put herself forward for partner.

2 — STATEMENT

Could be a killer stat – for example 99% of law firms say they'd like more women partners!

3 — QUESTION

"Have you ever wasted your end-of-year chat by avoiding the thorny subject of money?"

These are three powerful examples of something to get the audience thinking. Do you see how the content immediately hooks you into the subject?

It hooks the audience right through their faces. It's powerful to 'go there' yes, say it how it is.

In my experience as an Impact Guru who helps people make an impact and have the confidence to speak up, it's a waste of golden hook time if you start with a dull introduction.

You've probably heard this intro...

"Hello my name is 'insert name', and my job is 'insert boring job title and description of role."

Boring!

Research shows that people switch off after a few seconds if the subject doesn't grab them.

Believe me, when I was in broadcasting and we used to get 'overnights' to show you what the viewing figures were, you could literally see second by second when and possibly why your audience was switching off.

It's shocking and painful to know the truth about audiences.

An audience needs a quick fix fast.

Hook them!

TRIUMPHANT TIP

Engage your audience straight off... then talk from the heart, talk about what you know.

Fay Sharpe Founder FF15 / Chair of Trustees Muscle Help Foundation/ Founder Zibrant now part of BCD ME/Women's Advocate/ Mum of 2

CHAPTER 12
WHY STORIES REVEAL THE REAL YOU

Telling a story is the most engaging thing you can do when public speaking. There's science behind story telling. When you tell a story you light up parts of the brain that PowerPoint presentations just can't reach!

You and your audience can align your neural pathways! Hmm, oh yes, the same limbic part of your brain activates in the same way as your audience's brains when you tell a story – when you input an emotion or image.

Don't worry. You don't need to be a Hollywood scriptwriter to be able to tell stories – the easiest tip is this.

Think of a moment in your life. For example,

"I remember the time when _ "

Or

"I remember the conversation with xxxx (character) when she told me xxxxx"

A story could be a water-cooler moment or a moment when you were up all night ordering pizza with your colleagues because you were working on a pitch.

This rather goofy pic of me is about not being perfect. The story here is that I was getting ready to speak at a conference in London and I realised I needed a fresh black top to wear under my bright green (St Patrick's Day-style) jacket.

I was in a rush so I quickly got my iron out, turned up the heat and psssss – the sizzling sound and acrid smell was the give-away. I burnt a hole in my lovely black vest top.

Confession, I wore my dirty black vest from the day before inside out, so no one would notice the splodges of pancake batter down the front! Shhh don't tell anyone.

That day I looked like a swan, effortlessly speaking at the PA conference. Little did anyone know I had been paddling furiously underneath the water to get there!

I shared this story at one of my after-dinner keynotes and it was so easy to tell without a script because I had the prop (the offending vest) to show and tell!

This is a tiny moment, yet it has a great message – nobody's perfect. The great thing about stories like that is you don't need a script.

What's your story? I bet you have loads of stories up your sleeve. Perhaps you read an email in your inbox at 11pm at night? Were you in the middle of doing a deal with a client?

Try starting your story with... *"I remember the day when..."*

Go on, start telling your success stories to colleagues, family and friends and see what reaction you get.

Add in the location of the story, the description of the character you were talking to. Add senses – smells, sounds, and tastes if applicable.

Your story will allow your audience to join you on your emotional journey and they'll **LOVE** you for it.

Tell a story. I talk about tax so it's not that easy, but actually there is always a story to complement the cold hard facts.

Imagine roots under your feet – I find this thought process helps me slow down and centres me wherever and whenever I am talking (even if sitting down) so I can stand tall (or sit tall). Focus on your body language and have a strong and confident pose. Lose or reduce slides!

Zena Hanks, Partner for and on behalf of Saffery Champness LLP

CHAPTER 13
WHAT'S THE STORY, MORNING GLORY?

STORIES ARE AN EASY 'IN' FOR YOUR AUDIENCE TO GET TO KNOW YOU. A STORY ABOUT YOUR CAREER AND HOW YOU GOT TO BE DOING WHAT YOU DO IS FAR MORE COMPELLING THAN A LIST OF ACHIEVEMENTS.

I remember having a lightbulb moment at the BBC one morning during a live show. It changed my career. An agent, Tony, came into the studio with a guest one morning and piped up...

"Hey Esther, please can you give this man (the author) a personality? You are brilliant at helping dull people come to life on air, I've seen you work with the trickiest people like Theresa May."

(I had to agree the author was rather boring!)

"Yes!" I replied,

'Mr Dull' did spend the morning with me. He tried my practical formula and tips I had cultivated over my 20-year broadcasting career. He loved it, I loved it and yes, he did indeed get a personality worthy of his own TV series!

I couldn't stop thinking about what he said.

After work I went back to my flat and I had a long think over a glass of prosecco. And then it happened – I had a lightbulb moment!

That's it...I realised I had a very odd talent. I had a talent for showing people in their best light!

A few days later I created my "how to have a personality" formula for the first time. More on that later! Don't worry, you'll get all my best tips.

At that moment I realised I had created a fail-safe formula that could give (potentially dull) professionals a personality, not only on air, but in business: accountants, tax professionals, engineers, lawyers, internal audit chiefs and compliance people from global organisations and governments all over the world.

I dared to share my dream of leaving the BBC with my friend Tom, from Deloitte. He asked me about the formula and was blown away by it...

"Absolutely yes, people in business need your formula!" he enthused. But I had to make one of the hardest decisions of my life. Did I want to step outside my comfort zone and the SAFE 'golden handcuffs' and security of being a senior staffer at BBC?

Guess what? I did pluck up the courage to take a risk and jump from employee at the Beeb to setting up my own business. aarrgghh!

I left the BBC to help professionals build their charisma and have a personality. Now I'm known in the City as "The Impact Guru" and I travel the world speaking at events and working with execs from the USA and Canada, to Paris and Tel Aviv helping them to combat Glossophobia and have more impact, influence and confidence when they speak.

...and we all lived happily ever after.

The End.

Now your turn!

GET CRACKING

What short story could you tell very quickly to position you as an expert?

Your story could be as little as ten seconds if it's a quick memory. I suggest you have the ten second, 30 second, one-minute and three-minute version with more detail!

I created this story because at networking events people always ask me:

"What made you leave the BBC?"

This short story answers that question and also does lots of other things too. It...

– Positions me at the BBC

– Shows I'm credible in the City

– Has humour – it doesn't take itself too seriously

– Tells you about my background without me having to go into a lot of detail

– Explains why I decided to leave the BBC and become the Impact Guru

YOU have loads of stories up your sleeve, way more than you think.

Find a story or two that define moments in your career. That lightbulb moment. The project that went pear shaped and you had to fly to Luxembourg at midnight, or the board meeting that was cancelled at the last minute and you had to take over.

Make sure you have high-profile characters, organisations, numbers or locations, (Paris, NY) you can name drop, daaaaarling!

"There I was at the Film Festival in Cannes!" It doesn't have to be pretentious or showy. It just needs to position you as the expert, the leader or the pioneer.

It makes people **FEEL** something.

Go on, have a think.

You don't have to be perfect. It doesn't have to be a script, however it's relatively simple to write one and the most important thing is – it does a job. It tells you almost everything you need to know – **QUICKLY!**

CHAPTER 14
OBAMA TIPS YOU CAN'T RESIST

THE OBAMA DONUT TECHNIQUE

Former President of the USA, Barack Obama, is a very easy target to learn from and a joy to watch! His public speaking improved with time and I've learnt so much from his simple methods.

He was the master of the pause and the maestro of audience engagement. I spoke with one of Obama's speech writers and discovered he now uses a very simple technique to engage his audiences all over the world.

He used to have a 'master' speech – a generic one size fits all.

"We are going to change, we are going to look forward... etc"

He had holes in his speech ready to fill in the relevant gaps. Holes, hence the donut.

If his speech was about innovation and change, and he was speaking in London... he might say something like...

"When I come to London and see the Olympic park, I think, wow – that is innovation right there..."

"And when I met the Queen at Buckingham Palace I thought, you've managed to mix innovation with heritage..."

How can you steal this terrific little technique?

You fill the holes in the speech with local references.

For example. If you're talking to:

– senior management – you'd refer to their challenges ahead, the vision and even the KPIs.

– an audience of trainees and people under the age of 20, you might refer to social media or something that's in fashion right **NOW.**

Sometimes when you have a mixed audience you can divide them in half by the reference points. This is a good thing because you can acknowledge who they are so no-one feels left out, rather than pretend everyone knows what you're talking about.

For example, if I refer to a British TV programme like 'Sale of the Century' from the 1970s, (with Nicholas Parsons) half my audience over the age of 45 will laugh and clap, but anyone under 45 looks bemused and confused. I can make a joke of it, so the youngers can laugh at the olders reminiscing about an old retro programme! If most of the audience are younger, it wouldn't be a good idea to talk about it.

Use the donut technique and fill in the gaps and reference points that your audience will connect with.

It enhances and personalises your speech instantly.

The donut theory is short and sweet; all you have to do is fill the holes with sprinkles of audience-relevant references and anecdotes.

They'll love you for it!

Another fantastic trick from Obama is this easy-to-adopt tip to keep his audience engaged at all times: view and spew.

THE OBAMA VIEW AND SPEW METHOD

Obama liked speaking with a script. Maybe it was his 'security blanket'. I think I'd want one too if I was speaking to millions on television and to world leaders.

I admit it, I was one of those kids who found it hard to let go of my security blanket... even when I was six years old. And I see the same security blanket syndrome with my clients too. The other day my client said...

"I NEED a script." Really? Ok, I understand. Obama did too.

Having a script is like having a sucky blanket; it gives you security, which gives you confidence at your most vulnerable moment...in front of your multimillion-dollar client maybe! Or even worse, when you're presenting to your senior peers.

It's really hard to let the smelly tatty old blanky go, even though you know you should be grown up and oozing confidence.

Ideally, I'd LOVE it if you'd lose your script.

Why?

I like to see the whites of your eyes and I love it when you deliver your message as if you're the most relaxed and engaging person in the world – difficult if you're looking down and 'reading' lines.

Scripts can sound stilted, unnatural, too polite, not authentic and in most cases ...God forbid... **DULL.**

However, when you're under pressure, yes, I agree you need a safety net.

YOU NEED A SCRIPT!

If you **MUST** have a script then, please try and master this method. Obama couldn't memorise whole paragraphs of script. But he did do this and it worked like a charm... and you can too.

– He understood that he had to engage with his audience at **ALL** times. You need to engage! You need to show the audience with every fibre in your body that you care about **THEM.**

– Even now he still uses two transparent teleprompts (autocue screens) on either side of him so it appears as if he's looking at his audience to the right and to the left every few seconds. The tip here is – **LOOK UP** at **YOUR** audience at **ALL** times!

– He pauses while he memorises and 'views' the script for one or two sentences at a time, (notice he breathes through his nose to let the oxygen in slowly, another great tip you can adopt).

– Then he delivers these words out to the front, he 'spews' (he doesn't read and look down when he spews!).

– Note – this is more or less 15% viewing and 85% spewing straight out to the audience.

– And it **ALL** takes practice. (How much practice are you doing before a presentation?)

The next time you're pitching to clients or giving a high-level presentation, remember this...

Your script doesn't have feelings – it needs **NO** attention.

But **PEOPLE** do need attention.

And it connects them to you much faster.

TWO FOR ONE TIPS

Remember to breathe and smile simultaneously.

Charm the audience.

Reijo Oksanen, Director Ars Sacra, Helsinki

CHAPTER 15
HOW TO CREATE
INVISIBLE SAFETY NETS

My client Fi had to speak at a conference about a subject very close to her heart – her recovery from breast cancer. Her story was very moving, powerful and emotional and she'd told it hundreds of time before. She seriously knew her material and felt passionate about it.

I knew she was capable of smashing it!

Yet on this occasion, because it was on a proper conference stage with a grown-up podium and a 'Madonna' microphone, it was freaking her out.

She was seriously nervous because she HATED public speaking – you've spotted it – a Glossophobic. She described how she felt to me...

– Her legs go wobbly

– Her mind goes blank

– Light headed

– Sick to the stomach

These are all things I have experienced myself, and I knew I could help her because I have tried-and-tested tips and techniques.

The first thing I told her was, "It's ok, you are normal, you are just a bit nervous."

I shared my story of the first time I had full blown stage fright – when I was still at college – my first brush with Glossophobia. I had to do a five-minute stand-up comedy routine at university at the famous club 'Downstairs at the King's Head' Pub in Crouch End, London.

I remember feeling exactly like Fi and for three months, yes, three months, I could barely eat, sleep or think of anything else. I lost almost a stone in weight (6.3kg), I felt sick, worried and I had diarrhoea most days!

By the way, I wouldn't recommend that worry diet! It was a living nightmare.

Fi was much more mature than me (in my college days). She was well drilled on her story – she was well rehearsed - we even rehearsed it at her house.

She was well prepared and had written it out in full (just in case) – good! Tick that box.

However, she was still in that fearful **WHAT IF** mode. She was a worrier.

She started worrying about... well... everything...

What if my mind goes blank?

What if I shake?

What if I go red?

What if I sound like an idiot?

What if they HATE me?

What if I lose my credibility?

What if I stutter?

What if I fall over (Yes, I nearly did once)?

What if I repeat the same line over and over?

So I decided to go with her as moral support, help her warm up and do the power pose beforehand, talk her down, reassure and help her with my failsafe breathing exercises.

Fi was fine, she lived! Hurrah! The floor didn't open up, her mind didn't go blank, she was brilliant, the audience were moved to tears and ...phew, she nailed it. Woo hoo after all that worry – she was a warrior.

You too can go from worrier to warrior.

All you have to do is turn **WORRY** into **STRATEGY.**

GET CRACKING

Get a blank sheet of paper.

On the left write down your list of What ifs...

On the right write down your strategy.

It will help you put your mind at rest.

CHAPTER 16
DO YOU EXPERIENCE CREEPING DEATH?

Have you ever had a Creeping Death experience?

My client coined this phrase. It's the moment you get asked to introduce yourself round the meeting room table, like the grim reaper is coming to get you!

You know that feeling when you're asked, "Please introduce yourself round the table."

Everyone takes a turn and one by one gets picked off with their introduction.

This is probably what's going on in your head… (Cue the music…Under Pressure by Queen!)

Aarrgghh I wish the ground would open up, I hate this, I am not listening to anyone else, I am totally obsessed with the fact I am coming out in a rash and I don't know what to say… oh no, it's getting closer to my turn, oh no, I have nothing to say… What's my job title again? I can't remember what my job actually is… Oh sh*t ****, ****, it's only one person away, oh hell, I'm red, now I'm shaking, help help HELP…"

Sound familiar? I've been there too, yes, as you know, I wasn't born 100% confident.

I've had to work on strategies to gain confidence too.

First, this will make you laugh!

A TRUE CREEPING DEATH STORY

That May Make You Pee Yourself With Laughter.

One of my clients is very senior in a global bank. She's well respected and people 'think' she is completely confident and sure of herself because she is an outspoken and bubbly person who appears totally at ease at speaking in public – particularly round a boardroom table. However, she's secretly NOT at all confident and HATES that feeling of 'all the eyes are on me'.

She confessed to me that the last time they had a global 'summit' with senior people from all over the world, she did something she is totally ashamed of because she panicked.

There were about 40 very senior and influential people (including her, she is an influential person) sitting around the massive boardroom table on the top floor of the bank's HQ in London.

"Helen" arrived early to the meeting feeling ready to listen to the chairperson, but what she wasn't prepared for was the dreaded sentence...

"First, let's introduce ourselves around the table" ...aarrgghh at that moment, her heart jumped out of her mouth, she practically snorted her coffee and started to panic, pant, go red, sweat. She literally had that moment of *'fight, flight or freeze'.* Her natural instinct at that moment was *'flight'.*

She looked at where she was sitting and in her blind panic calculated that she was around number 32 out of 40 and it would take approx. 30 seconds for each person to introduce themselves – therefore she had approx 16 minutes to do something drastic. She stood up, excused herself (as if she was going to the ladies) and as quick as a flash, vanished into the 'client' corridor where all the catering staff were busying themselves with the morning refreshments.

It was 11am.

She followed one of the waiters into the main catering kitchen. The lovely Spanish manager saw this very high-profile and smart-looking woman and asked very politely,

"Can I help you with anything, Madam?"

With that, Helen blurted out *"Can I buy a glass of wine now?"*

Looking confused, the catering manager glanced at his watch (it was 11am).

"Um, we don't sell wine by the glass, we sell it by the bottle only!"

Helen couldn't think of anything dignified to say at this point and carried on with her quest.

"Ok, that's fine, I'll take a bottle of white please, quick as you can!"

"All we have chilled is the Chablis, it's £22 at cost" he replied.

"Fine, I'll take the bottle."

With that, the catering manager went to the fridge and brought out the Chablis. Luckily it had a screw top, so it was easy to open.

Helen pointed at one of the wine glasses on the trolley, and the catering manager got the message and passed it to her as he watched in horror as she opened the bottle right there in front of him.

She poured herself a **LARGE** (over 250ml) fish-bowl sized glass of Chablis and proceeded to gulp it down in one go. She left the rest of the bottle, slammed it down on the trolley and ran out shouting,

"I'll pay you after the meeting!"

She ran back into the large boardroom for her **'creeping death'** experience and she'd only been gone eight minutes so she had around eight minutes left to compose herself with her now slightly rosy cheeks and possibly the odd hiccup!

She didn't hear one word of what anyone else had to say, or who they were, and concentrated on her job description and *'survival'* techniques.

When I asked her how it went – she told me she couldn't remember a thing. She must have wiped it from her memory, she went on autopilot, and she had an out-of-body experience. It felt like it wasn't even her in the room – someone had taken over her body.

Apparently, she totally forgot to pay for her bottle of Chablis – oops!

At this point, I'd like to make it very clear that my top tip is **DO NOT** drink alcohol! Tee hee, it will **NOT** help you. 'Dutch Courage' is absolutely **NOT** a good idea, believe me I've tried. Alcohol may make your mouth dry, it may stop you from thinking clearly, and at worst it will make you slur your speech. A lazy drunken tongue is **NOT** a credible style!

Yes I have tried **EVERY** single tip when it comes to public-speaking confidence and nerves.

Here's what I shared with Helen... if she ever gets herself in that 'creeping death' scenario again, here's what she's going to do... and you too!

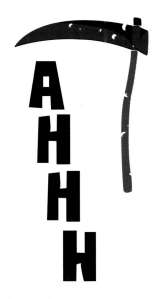

– **Don't panic!**

– **Don't drink booze**

– **DO breathe, it will be fine**

– **DO have a pre-thought-through 'elevator-pitch' – spiel!**

This is something you can work on any time when you're totally relaxed.

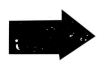 

★ TEASER TIP ★

Don't drink alcohol for public-speaking courage – it DOESN'T work on any occasion! Seriously I've tried it.

Me.

CHAPTER 17

WHAT IF MY MIND GOES BLANK??

I remember that moment you dread. It was one of my earlier speaking engagements in London.

I was asked to speak at a 'Women in Data' event at Deloitte.

It was pretty nerve-racking as one of the more senior leaders was in the room. So it probably spooked a few of the group and they seemed quite quiet. Of course, I thought it was me.

At the time I remember thinking "Do they hate this? They seem a bit quiet."

Then I started to overthink everything and doubt myself halfway through my sentences.

Then it happened...

My mind went blank! Aarrgghh.

Oops, I literally (for a few seconds) went totally blank!

Luckily, I remembered my safety net.

I asked the audience a question or said something like,

"Have a think about that"

I wandered over to the side table where my water and notes were, took a sip of water (great tip, it buys you a second or four), and there I had my running order with my key points written down.

In my haze of slight panic I couldn't read the whole page, so I just saw the first thing on the sheet and it triggered the next bit of my talk.

Phew – that was my 'Get out of jail free' card that saved me from total failure.

And guess what – no one noticed.

I LOOKED OVER MY NOTES AND I COULD SEE I HAD MISSED OUT A WHOLE CHUNK OF CONTENT — ABOUT 15 MINUTES!! OOPS, DO YOU THINK THE AUDIENCE NOTICED? OF COURSE THEY DIDN'T!

It's exactly the same as when I worked in TV at the BBC – you sweat and sweat in the edit suite to get the perfect shot and audio. You beat yourself up if you cut out the "brilliant" part of the interview because there was background noise of a drill in the road.

Does the audience know you cut out the best quote?

No, the audience only knows what you tell them, not what you leave out.

Here are three examples of handy safety nets...

SAFETY NET 1 – KEEP A SCRIPT NEARBY.

In my case – one on the floor, one at the side by the water and one under the laptop shelf of the podium – I had three dotted around in that instance. **IT WORKED.**

SAFETY NET 2 – HAVE AN ANCHOR.

You can have a safety one-liner which has worked for me and my clients in the past.

Have a picture in your mind that would be relevant – e.g. I had a picture of an inspiring teacher at my high school in London...

"I remember meeting Mrs Prodan at Ellen Wilkinson High School in Ealing and her advice to me was _ ."

SAFETY NET 3 — NAME YOUR CONTENT CHUNKS.

I find it useful to name my content chunks and each piece is a visual image, eg The Power POSE, the combatting nerves exercise, the 60% issue, etc. These trigger a whole 15-minute sequence.

So my notes might look like this:

POSE

Nerves

60%

Yours might be pictures, icons, smily faces – anything that will jog your imagination.

A friend of mine shared with me her trick of using images of lily pads with her key words in them – so she can seamlessly jump from one to the next like a little frog!

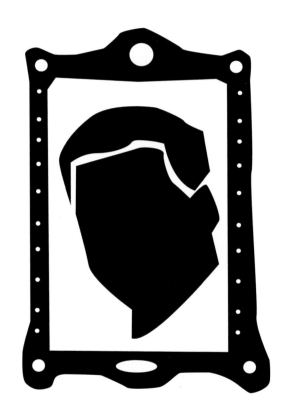

134

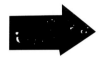

TONGUE—IN—CHEEK TIP

Place or hold a favourite picture of a family member (a friendly face) next to your script. Remember to look at it from time to time when you start to get nervous.

Priscilla Kim Lo, Financial Services Professional, New York

CHAPTER 18
WHAT IF I GO RED?

"How do I avoid going red?"

"What do I do about my rash?"

These are two of the most common questions I get asked by Glossophobics!

The going red phenomenon seems to be spreading – and as they say in the USA it's one of the *'non-verbal leakage'* issues!

Yes, it's one of the tell-tale signs that you are nervous before you've even spoken.

One of my clients at Deloitte used to wear a scarf every day, all year round.

When I met her she had on a really lovely blue scarf, in fact she told me she had half a wardrobe full of fashionable scarves because she was worried on a daily basis – in meetings, in presentations, with clients and at networking events – that she "might go red or break out in the rash at any moment".

Wow, that must be stressful, living in fear every day!

In a meeting the first thing she would feel was a little flushed (who doesn't) then she'd feel the rosy-red heat spread from her cleavage (décolletage) and slowly work its way up to her neck. It would reach her chin and then often, aarrgghh, her face!

She told me it was getting worse, hence the scarf strategy.

I must admit, she did wear her scarf pretty high up.

She was really embarrassed about this 'rash' and she felt terrible.

I told her not to worry because many more of my clients had come out with their 'rash stories'.

Yikes! One poor woman was on camera making video clips for a top law firm and, when we watched the footage, she looked as if she was wearing a camouflage body suit.

She was wearing a sleeveless dress and the strange shaped patches were her skin. Her nervousness on camera had brought her out in a full body rash and no make-up, powder or foundation would cover that up.

When your mind goes blank your body is reacting to fear, which leads to anxiety, which leads to your heart rate going up, which creates cortisol, (the stress hormone) which leads to side effects!

How to stop going beetroot red!

TIP 1 — BLOW OUT THE CANDLES — SMELL THE ROSES

THIS IS A ONE-MINUTE OPTION!

Breathe – slow breathing (as if you are in labour, yes it reduces pain too). 10 beats blowing out the candle and 8 beats smelling the roses is an instant winner, which immediately reduces your heart rate.

It literally takes 45 seconds to get rid of cortisol – that's under a minute!

This is the most effective option for a quick fix! It worked a treat for my scarf-wearing client.

The scary option – Let it go! Don't fight it.

Let your body go red, have a rash, feel the tingly rush of blood to your face.

Don't fight it and say to yourself "It's OK, here comes the rash!"

I have tried this and it **WORKS** – I have let myself go red, get sweaty, go blank and guess what? It passes. It doesn't take long to pass either when you don't fight it.

TIP 2
—THE LONG—TERM OPTION. PRACTISE, PRACTISE, PRACTISE.

The more you speak, the more you get used to it and the more your body won't react.

Do **NOT** avoid public speaking at all costs; do it more. Start small and speak to groups of three then four then five and so on. It's the long-term anti-blushing formula.

Remember the golden rule? The audience doesn't care about you! The audience only cares about what's in it for them.

They don't care that much if you go red and they might even find it endearing. If you don't make it into a big deal, they won't.

This takes the pressure off you. Concentrate on them rather than you and then you're halfway there.

"HELLO TREACLE" TIP

Close your eyes in front of a mirror (only briefly) and envisage you're a sparkling Hollywood star like Catherine Zeta-Jones or Angelina Jolie. Open your eyes holding that thought –

You'll feel a million dollars!

**Melinda Leigh
founder of Nirvana Chocolate**

CHAPTER 19

WHAT IF I SOUND LIKE AN IDIOT?

The answer to this question is...
YOU WON'T...
if you focus on the right things!
(And read this book!)

However, if you want to be 'perfect' and
'correct' and never say anything 'wrong',
you are in danger of holding yourself back.

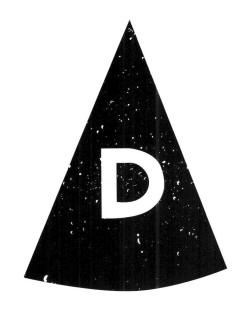

One of my media clients, Laurel, who is very high up in HR, confessed to me when we first met...

"I completely avoid putting myself in a position where I might sound like an idiot."

"That's fantastic, what's your secret?" I asked.

She assured me confidently.

"I never speak in public or in meetings unless I'm 100% prepped,"

"Aarrhhh OK, and how often do you speak up?"

... "Never"

That was before she met me and before I persuaded her that she didn't need to be perfect! But she DID need to be visible.

Can you relate to Laurel?

You can't be perfect and correct **ALL** the time – certainly when you're public-speaking. So if you can get your head around this – you're going to fly!

A BIG shortcut to this 'what if' is to make sure you prep with the focus on the **AUDIENCE – NOT** yourself. Yes, this is a big theme of this book.

Because it works!

If you want the audience to say "Oh, brilliant" then give you a standing ovation, you can do this.

THE MAIN THING IS TO TRANSFER YOUR WORRY AND MAKE IT INTO A STRATEGY.

Remember the audience doesn't care about you, they only care about themselves. So make sure you are giving them something THEY care about.

YOU'LL BE IDIOT-PROOF IF YOU:

– Think about what the audience NEEDS to know and what stories they might LIKE to hear.

– Don't worry about your inhibitions, and put them to one side for the moment. Your worry about sounding like an idiot is your voice of doubt. As you've heard me say before "Shut it out – be quiet, Cyril!" (That's what my voice of doubt is called.)

– Concentrate on having a message that's relevant to the audience.

– Interview one of your potential audience members, or someone who knows the audience you're going to be in front of. Ask them about what the audience might like to know and what they care about.

– If you think the people in the audience are 'cleverer' than you, great. Use their expertise by asking them their thoughts and opinions about the subject ahead of time. In my experience "clever" people like the sound of their own voice.

– You don't need to know EVERYTHING in the whole world. How can you?

– It feels risky to stand in front of people 'in case you make a fool of yourself'. But there's a greater risk when you aren't willing to stand up and speak out…

– The risk that you are invisible and unmemorable (and you lose out on opportunities because people don't see you express yourself).

TONNES OF TIPS

1. Rehearse until the mirror cracks.

   Audiences know when you are winging it.

2. Don't ever ever skip slides (if you use them).

   Shows the content wasn't meant for the audience in

   the room.

3. If you use props, rehearse with them.

4. Always use a remote clicker, and the blackout button at

   least once during the show.

5. Move on the stage only when you want to move

   the audience.

Barnaby Wynter,
Keynote Speaker, Author, Business Writer

CHAPTER 20
WHAT IF I SHAKE?

Have you ever seen someone hold a page of notes that quivers uncontrollably? Given that Glossophobia is much more common than you think, I bet you have!

I have, and I have had the shakes myself.

Have you ever seen a business presentation or wedding speech where the person you thought was super-confident is shaking? You see their perfectly typed script on a perfectly white sheet start to quiver. It's brutal. A4 paper doesn't hide a shaking hand.

I remember being shocked at my friend's wedding. Her usually confident and outspoken dad quivered and shook his way through his wedding speech with his flimsy A4 sheet of white paper – perfectly scripted.

I remember thinking...

If only he'd:

– put his script down on the table and not held it in his shaky hand

– done a quick warm up to calm himself down

– breathed for 45 seconds – my special blow out the candles trick

– used thicker card stock instead of paper

I wish I'd had a chance to give him a few tips before he spoke.

He could have turned **Worry into Strategy.**

If you shake?

First of all, if you read this pocket book and practise all the tips, you are unlikely to shake.

Hurray, that's great news!

Let's go back to basics.

You are likely to shake if your heart rate goes up suddenly. Why would your heart rate go up suddenly? Because you are **SCARED! AARRGGHH** and **NERVOUS AARRGGHH!**

You might have Glossophobia, but the good news is, you can combat the side effects.

My Harley Street therapist buddy, Olivia James, shared her physiological explanation for Glossophobia and why your body may shake.

When you are in this state of fight or flight, basically your entire nervous system shuts down or goes nuts. This could cause you to shake.

The longest nerve in your body, your vagus nerve (nothing to do with Vegas!), tells your body to do all sorts of disgusting things.

Maybe your tummy wants to vomit or your mind goes blank because the frontal cortex of your brain can't function.

It's normal. Your nervous system is there to help you survive as a human being. If you are in great danger, a life or death situation, your body reacts. The trouble with Glossophobia is that it's not life or death but your brain reacts in the same way unless you untrain it to react like that.

When your nervous system starts shutting down, all bets are off. It doesn't matter how clever you are, or how brilliant your script is. You need to get your physiological state back to normal.

If you prepare in the right way and have a strong message, know your audience and have done absolutely everything in your power to be mentally and physically ready – you are much less likely to shake.

GET CRACKING

– No hand-held microphone

– Use a lapel microphone, or no microphone

– No notes in your hand – put your note on the table or podium in front of you

– If you don't have a table – where possible move furniture!

– No pens or markers! Get someone else to write on the flip chart – it's so much better for you to be giving the audience attention anyway

– No A4 flimsy paper – if you MUST have notes, have HARD card

– In TV we had 'idiot boards' i.e. big boards you could have at the back of the room or on the floor with your notes on them

– "What if I shake?"

You won't – **DONE!**

TRUTHFUL TIPS

Remember it is only you that knows what you intended to say. I found this really helpful in not worrying about making sure everything was covered, and as long as all the key points were made in a clear way, I didn't need to beat myself up.

Anon – Senior Banker

CHAPTER 21

WHAT IF I HAVE A WARDROBE MALFUNCTION?

My client's email made me laugh out loud as I was stuck on the tube, at Bank Station in London, the other day.

Thank you Ms X for sharing your major presentation wardrobe malfunction with us. You will remain anon!

I got some strange looks when I burst out laughing. OK, I may have snorted!

This is what it said...

"If you decide to wear power heels, watch out for holes in the floor.

I was unable to move for a full five minutes due to a stiletto incident.

Fortunately, I'm not one of those lapel mics, confidently-working-the-space types. I was tucked behind the lectern.

I did, however, have to reach down and pull my shoe out of the floor with both hands at the end of my presentation, so it can't have escaped notice. PS: no shoes were harmed."

Thank you again, Ms X, and I'm glad to hear your heels weren't harmed!

Well that's a first – I love it.

Heels can be precarious at the best of times.

I find wedges are a good compromise if you want to avoid spiking floors, too much "clip clop" noise or looking too wobbly.

(Remember the power of the pose?) You need to feel sturdy on stage. That goes for you too gents!

And what about other garments?

Careful of those unsightly sweat patches (British Prime Minister Tony Blair had a sweaty shirt crisis at the Labour Party conference in 2000 – oops). One of my lovely blue jackets let me down badly once – I had to chuck it out because it showed dark circles around the arm pits – eeew. Yes embarrassing, when you're speaking in front of 120 lawyers at a posh hotel!

To make sure you **NEVER** suffer from heel in the floor or sweat patch hell, I asked for some tips from my fabulous expert stylist guru Natasha Musson, who dresses hundreds of execs every year.

```
****************************************
*                                      *
*         NATASHA'S TOP 5              *
*    HOW—TO—AVOID—WARDROBE             *
*      —MALFUNCTION TIPS:              *
*                                      *
****************************************
```

1. TAILORING AND FIT IS CRUCIAL.

Avoid any garment that is too tight and could reveal underwear underneath, which could distract your audience. If your skirt, dress, trousers or collar feel tight it will affect the way you stand.

You don't want to adjust your clothes on stage, which will make you look nervous. (And no hands in pockets please!)

Choose an outfit that fits you perfectly, that you have worn before and feel fantastic in.

(You know you look well put together.)

Remember the 2 Cs Comfortable = Confidence

2. BEWARE...

– a raised stage (avoid short skirts, arrhh, too much thigh IS distracting).
– mismatched socks.
– shoes that are too high – practise walking in heels
– leaving price stickers on your soles (my pet hate)

3. CHOOSE YOUR FABRIC CAREFULLY.

– Go for natural, breathable fabrics like cotton, and avoid silks and polyester that
  you are likely to sweat in.
– Keep the style simple.
– When trying on your outfit, practise standing up and sitting down in a mirror
  to double-check the fabric doesn't easily crease.

4. INJECT A SPLASH OF COLOUR INTO YOUR OUTFIT.

– Avoid boring white shirts/blouses and wear something that shows your character. For
me (Natasha), that would be red lipstick and some great earrings; for Esther that would be
a fabulous necklace and a quirky pair of shoes. This reveals the 'real you' in a subtle way and
you'll be yourself and be more likely to smile.

Thank you, Natasha for the great advice. I have one thing to add!

My big bonus tip:

5. DO A DRESS REHEARSAL IN THE SAME VENUE!

Do a recce (a reconnaissance – you know, a military approach to checking what you're dealing with). The venue, the stage, the lights, the steps, the temperature of the room.

Will you sweat if you wear a thick shirt under a thick jacket?

Is the floor noisy – are there steps up to a stage?

Remember my story? About speaking at the International Edinburgh TV festival about Rapture TV (before my BBC days). My skirt was too tight to step up onto the stage – I had to lift it up so my legs could move! Fail.

Remember – always turn worry into strategy.

You'll be absolutely fine.

Get there early! Be enthusiastic – be eager to share.

Will Kintish – Speaker and author of 'Business Networking – The Survival Guide'

CHAPTER 22
HOW TO OVERCOME FEAR

163

So you're afraid of looking stupid, breaking out in a rash, losing your cool and looking a fool in front of your peers?

Or one of your worst nightmares... being **CRITICISED** by the people you respect.

You think that if you fail, this could HURT you. It will seep into every pore and ruin your life FOREVER. Aarrgghh!

One of my clients shared her public speaking story with me the other day. She bombed so badly. At the beginning of her talk her mind went blank and she sobbed in front of the very senior medical faculty of a top university in England! Ouch.

Then she attempted to avoid any speaking engagement like the plague for as long as she could (yes, years). So when she was asked to chair a meeting (because she was very senior and she couldn't hide any more) she had to ask her doctor to prescribe her with Diazepam (Valium)!

She had worked herself up into a frenzy of self-doubt, imposter syndrome, panic and self-sabotage. I told her – it's OK, you're not alone; you have classic Glossophobia. Most people feel like this. I used to feel this way and I turned a corner and learnt to overcome my fear.

I'll help you overcome Glossophobia. Just like Ms Diazepam did!

Don't worry, you don't need to be 100% perfect.

You are going to overcome anxiety and you are going to LOVE standing up and speaking to your clients, your colleagues and your seniors at work. Trust me.

First, let's understand why you have this fear, this shaking, this uncontrollable urge to dig a hole and climb into it.

As you know, scientists call this the 'fight or flight' reaction where your body goes into survival mode. Back in the Stone Age, this extreme reaction to threat and fear would have saved your life. Humans are built to sense fear and 'Get outta here!'

It's OK; it's common for your mind to go blank! Classic stage fright – Glossophobia. If you've experienced it, it's OK, you probably won't have to again because here's the good news... there is a cure.

QUITE SIMPLY YOUR HEART RATE WENT UP AND YOU NEED TO GET IT BACK DOWN!

My very good friend, Nicola Fox, is a hypnotherapist. She has a theory about why we have this irrational HATRED of public speaking...

Glossophobia is such a strong fear for so many people because, as well as being about a lack of control, it's about the risk of rejection by our 'tribe'. 'Tribes' can be our work colleagues, family, friends or audience – in fact, any group important to us.

We are social creatures, evolved to live in groups for support and protection. For early humans, being outcast by our 'tribe' exposed us to danger and put our survival in jeopardy.

Now, although our lives don't actually depend on it, the possibility of publicly making a mistake, being humiliated, shamed or rejected is a powerful deterrent.

PRACTISE PRACTISE PRACTISE

- Yeah, yeah, yeah Mum!

Even if you're not a planner, and you like off-the-cuff freestyle, don't wing it!

Leave winging it for the chickens!

Practice makes perfect – of course it does – your mum told you that.

In my experience practicing and then just going for it has reduced my fear by 90%.

But this isn't just practicing a 'script'.

First, practise standing, and speaking such as telling a simple joke in front of your family. Start with 2 people, then 3 then 4 and so on – but you must do it standing up.

Start small. Little steps. But DO start.

Standing up feels odd at first but it will soon feel normal.

Go there, yes, step outside your comfort zone.

Plan a teeny tiny speaking 'gig' TODAY – yes even at your family gathering this weekend. Or your next team meeting.

OK, so stage fright happens when you are in 'fight or flight' mode – **panic aarrgghh.**

It's OK, you get this when your heart rate goes up.

Other side effects when your heart rate goes up;

– Rash

– Shaking

– You go white

– You go blank

– You lose your speech

All really useful conditions if you're trying to come across as confident, credible and with gravitas (Not!).

All you need is to get rid of the cortisol (stress hormone) in your body. It can take under a minute to do this.

GET CRACKING

Plan a really easy speaking 'gig' TODAY – yes even at your family gathering this weekend. Or your next team meeting. Even three to four people. Make sure you stand up and deliver a short story or go through a few slides. Go on, you can do it.

CHAPTER 23
WARM UP YOUR INSTRUMENT!

Me with alto sax at age 18 for a college rock band photo shoot in the late 1980s, taken by Jason Buck.

OK, I agreed to 'model' for this this photo shoot with my alto sax when I was in a college rock bank called 'The Great Pagoda Dream Factory'. It was named after the famous Pagoda building in Kew Gardens in West London near my college.

It's not just for show – I did complete all my music grades up to 8 and played in five different groups including the Ealing Young Musicians orchestra and a Glenn Miller swing band.

I did one gig with the 1980s group 'Curiosity Killed the Cat' – now that's another story for another book altogether!

One thing's for sure – when it comes to tuning up and warming up – **YOU MUST DO IT!**

Warming up, just like with an orchestra, must happen way before the 'curtain up' moment.

When I played my saxophone, it would take around five minutes to warm up my instrument so it didn't sound flat.

So here's the tip, you must warm up your instrument – that's you – your body is your instrument!

A great way to help **FEEL** up for it, is to get yourself physically up for it.

Don't worry – you're not doing this in front of anyone!

Physically moving around and making yourself feel happy helps you overcome nerves.

There's not one downside to warming up. OK, you want your heart rate to come down, yes, but you want your nerve endings, voice and physicality to be "ready for action".

An athlete warms up their muscles before a race. Actors get to the theatre early to do both a group and an individual warm-up.

There's literally no downside.

You can get your heart rate down later.

Do whatever makes you feel good to warm up your body; dance around the room – do the mashed potato – we used to do this with the production team in the BBC studio before we went live on air.

Or you could walk, jog on the spot or even do the Haka (you know, the famous ritual dance the New Zealand rugby team, the All Blacks, do before each game… all together now 'Huh'!).

One of my clients recently did the Haka three times in Portland Place in London (by the Langham Hotel), when he had to go to an assessment centre for his promotion at one of the big four accounting firms.

He confessed to me that his biggest worry was that he would lack energy throughout the day – which started at 8am with a gruelling schedule of panel interviews, pitching his business case, an off-the-cuff presentation with Q&A after the coffee break, then two role-plays after lunch.

Phew – that's a long day and really, really stressful.

I asked him what his favourite physical booster would be and he said,

"I can do the Haka."

He decided to go into the street (down a side street I hope) and do the Haka in each break.

Guess what – it worked!

GET CRACKING

Pick your favourite dance, jig, walk, wiggle or any physical movement that fills you with energy. Do this for 2 minutes. You don't literally want to break into a sweat, but you do want to warm your body up! You will feel much more prepared when it's time to speak and much more energised!

CHAPTER 24
DON'T THINK ABOUT THE AUDIENCE BEING NAKED!

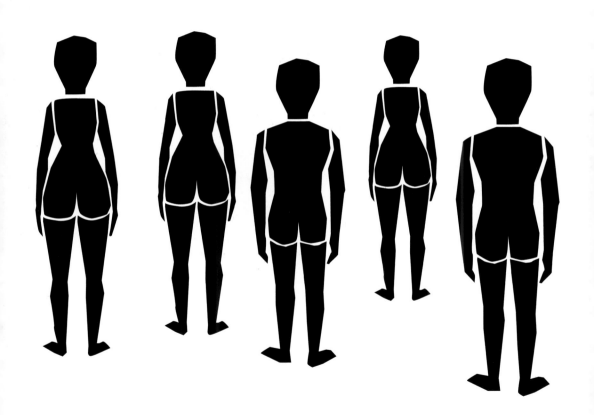

The worst advice I've **EVER** been given? *"Think of your audience naked."*

DO NOT DO THAT.

I remember at my kids' speech day at school in London, the head girl gave a hilarious speech about how she didn't know how to prep her big day at the podium. I felt for her. She was very poised but clearly quite nervous. Seriously brave, she was only 13.

She went through all the advice her teachers, parents, grandad and friends had given her including ...

"Just imagine the audience are naked, and you'll be fine."

Of course, this went down a treat with an auditorium full of 4-13 year olds!

She got a huge laugh (that's a real coup for a 13-year-old, well done)

Her verdict?

"It doesn't work!"

Just like the head girl, I have also tried imagining the audience naked.

It doesn't work. Although I understand the sentiment. The audience isn't scary, – they are bare-naked human beings that you can laugh at versus strong powerful judges who may laugh at you.

Beware – this is one massive distraction. And you don't want to be internally laughing at your audience.

It totally puts you off, although if it makes you laugh I'll give it a tiny weeny bit of merit.

Here's what really helps you – Visualise Success.

GET CRACKING

Imagine this during practice as well as the night before and the day of the event:

– The audience loves your speech.

– They give you a standing ovation because what you are saying is so powerful.

– You feel happy and relaxed on stage as you effortlessly crack jokes and make the audience laugh and smile.

See? That's much more helpful than the naked image! Ewwwwww.

DO visualise how brilliant you are going to look, sound and feel on stage and capture that thought for a few seconds as many times as you can.

CHAPTER 25
SPEAK TO ONE!

Remember the late, great TV presenter in the UK, Cilla Black?

She was well known for having an intimate relationship with 18.2 million TV viewers in the late 1980s on her popular ITV show Blind Date.

Her trick, and one you can use, is that she used to call her camera "Bobby" after her late husband. She LOVED her Bobby more than anything in the world, therefore she loved her camera, hence 18.2 million people thought she loved them. They could feel her love and affection oozing from the TV screen.

She'd say in her Scouse accent it's the Liverpudlian accent – you would recognise it from The Beatles. *"Bring Bobby over here"*.

The tip 'Speak to one' has been a game changer for me and many of my clients.

A senior partner at a global law firm used this technique and won the big vote for chair!

So think of the person who can represent your audience and give them a name. Preferably make it someone you know and love very much, someone who has a sense of humour and who'd be championing you and urging you to do well.

Imagine them standing right there with a drink as if you are at the bar laughing and joking. The more intimate and familiar you are, the better.

In fact, the more formal the presentation or speech, the more conversational you need to be.

Always say 'you' rather than 'everyone in the room' or 'you out there'.

Talking to "YOU" and only "YOU" is one of the most powerful public speaking tools I've learnt!

You'll love it. See I'm talking to you, sshhh, no one else knows about this, just you!

TENACIOUS TIPS

– Own the stage.

– Use pauses for dramatic effect.

– Use blank screens to wake up
a dozy audience.

– Speak slower than you
normally would.

**Martin Robinson,
Risk & Audit Consultant, UK**

CHAPTER 26
THE POWER OF THE POSE

THIS IS THE ULTIMATE GLOSSOPHOBIA—BASHER — IT'S PHYSICAL, IT'S QUICK AND IT WORKS SUPER FAST!

All those years spent taking nervous contributors in the live BBC studio from anxious to awesome, in a matter of moments, taught me this simple physical formula.

I've boiled down the essential speaking tips for you to help you become a little bit brilliant at speaking in under two minutes!

THE POWER OF THE POSE

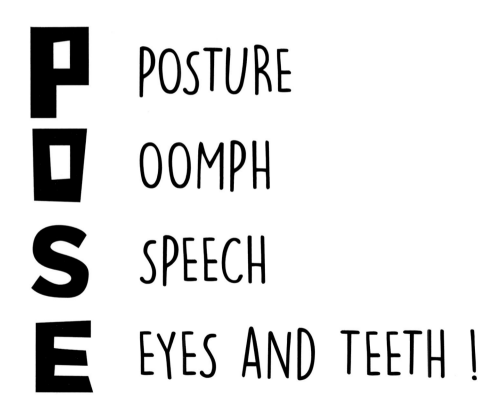

P POSTURE

O OOMPH

S SPEECH

E EYES AND TEETH !

Body language – and, as they say in America, the 'non-verbals' – are what make you awesome.

The way you look, sound and feel are KEY – you've got to be awesome so the whole thing comes together.

This is the fun bit.

I've left the awesome piece for the end of this book because the non-verbal body language, and what the audience sees, help you inside and out... i.e.

– What do you do with hands?

– What do you do with your feet?

– What does your posture say about you?

– Why is 'eyes and teeth' so important?

– How do you maximise your voice?

– Is an accent a problem?

Being awesome is the rich and beautiful icing on your public speaking cake.

This **WILL** make you into a successful public speaker – however you've got to do all the groundwork first.

Being the producer behind the glass of the BBC studio, and giving all my on-air talent quick-fix coaching lessons, transformed them and me. I realised there were four easy-to-adopt physical things you can do to make you AWESOME in an instant!

I always advise my clients to watch Professor Amy Cuddy's famous TED Talk about the power of the POSE and the science behind body language for an extra confidence fix.

I am proud to say I came up with my little **POSE** mnemonic years ago because it's an instant shortcut to speaking success in any situation. (In fact, my siblings say I always had my hands on my hips trying to boss them around!)

I've been spreading the **POSE** formula all over the world in boardrooms, meeting rooms, job interviews, conference podiums and pitches.

The good news – it's easy and takes only seconds!

It's time to master the power **POSE!** How is your posture?

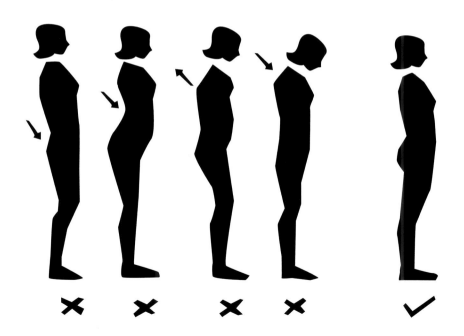

POSTURE! Sit up children. Come on, sit up straight. Yes I do mean you! Can you straighten your back as you read this?

I remember sitting in assembly at school with Mrs Dunnington. She'd remind us each day to sit up straight with a "nice straight back".

"Look at Lisa Kent, see how straight her back is." (I was jealous of Lisa Kent.)

The point is that standing and sitting up straight is **ABSOLUTELY** essential to your confidence, your voice, your status and your gravitas.

Adjusting your posture will help you look, sound and feel confident in a matter of seconds. There's no downside to this tip.

In Professor Amy Cuddy's famous TED Talk she talks about power posing for two minutes in order to build up your testosterone! Yes, the hormone that encourages bold and confident behaviour!

MY POSTURE TIP IS MORE ABOUT YOUR PRESENCE, STATUS AND VOICE

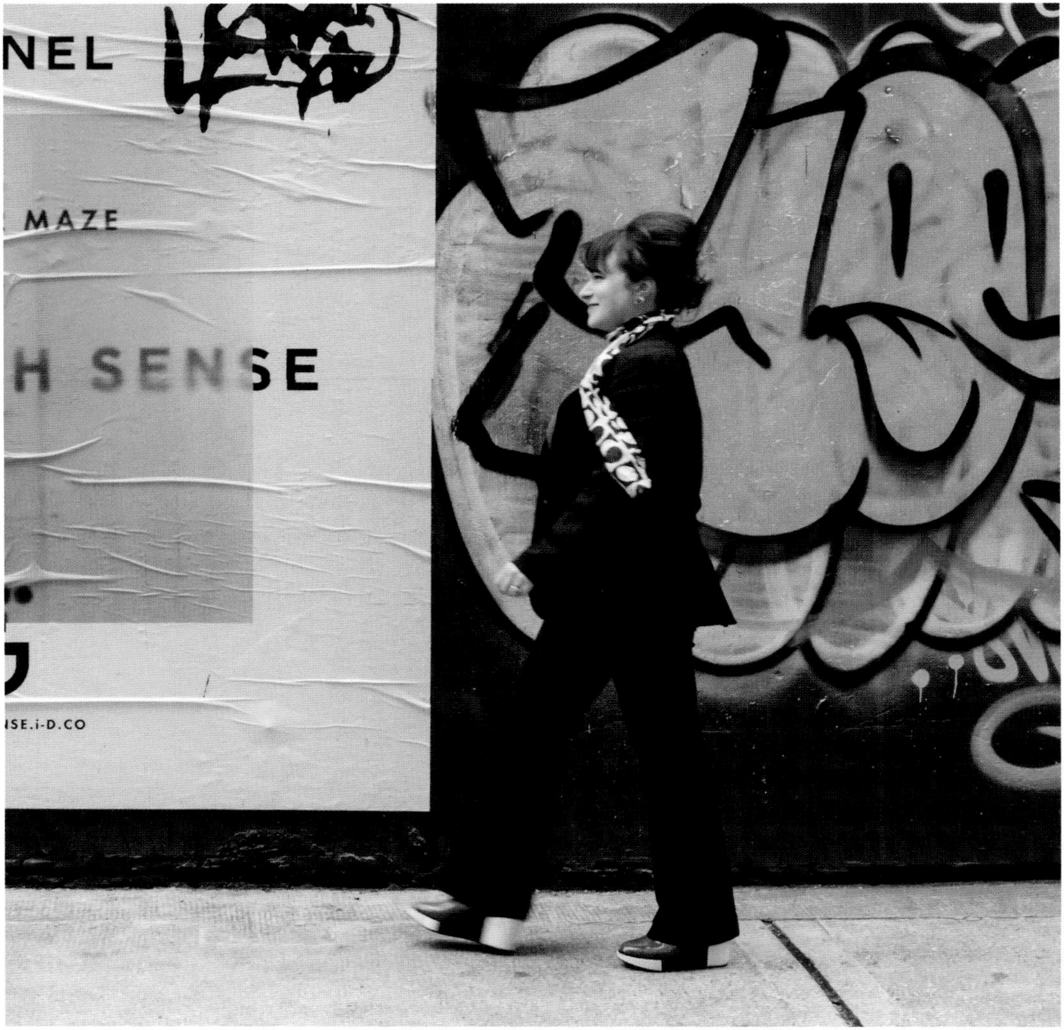
NEL
MAZE
H SENSE
NSE.i-D.CO

I remember one of my clients from a global professional services firm in London; let's call him "Kris."

He had been given feedback in his mock panel interview when he was being promoted to a director. Here's what the senior people interviewing him had originally said about his interview performance.

Brace yourself.

"Kris had a good business case but in the Q&A he looked as if he was up against the ropes in a boxing ring waiting for the next punch."

Ouch! That hurt.

Luckily for Kris, he had the opportunity to work with me on his confidence in the Q&A and stage presence before panel interview round 2 – ding ding!

The first thing I did was film him doing a few mock questions (yes I know, painful but it's the fastest way of learning and I always make it fun not judgemental).

The one thing Kris needed to nail in his interview was a **POWERFUL POSTURE!**

Literally that was it. Oh yes and a smile – more on that later.

So we did a special posture warm-up. You can try this too.

Whatever makes you feel powerful:

– Arms up as if you've won a race

– Hands on hips like Wonder Woman!

– Shake your body to get rid of tension

– Jump up and down to get more energy

– Stand tall

You've probably done this in yoga, Pilates or at the gym...

– Feet hip-width apart

– Legs straight but not locked

– Crown of the head stretching up towards the ceiling

– "Grow an inch in height", I'd say

– Arms loose (hands coming up don't worry)

Kris would hunch and lean back when he was under pressure. However,with an awareness of his posture, he rose to the challenge.

He looked so much more confident when he stood or sat up straight.

The idea is to take up as much physical space as you possibly can.

I encouraged Kris to fill out as much space as he could...

No leaning, crossing the body, curving the spine or tilting the head. Any physical sign that shows you are shrinking will reduce your gravitas and status instantly.

BIG
BIG
BIG
TALLER

So think BIG, BIG, BIG – TALLER than you can possibly be.

OK, if you have back issues or can't stand tall for some reason, you can mentally take up your space – claim your space in the room or at that table.

Before our sessions Kris was showing with his body language that he was uncomfortable, and he was almost asking permission to take up the space. He was physically and non-verbally apologising for the space he was taking up.

"Go on Kris," I'd urge, "Go on, sit up straight, as tall as you can be and smile."

It totally transformed the way he performed and guess what?

He got the promotion.

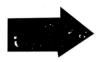

TREE
TIP

Plant your feet, so you don't sway.
Imagine you're a tree
trunk and your roots
are running through your
feet into the floor.

Me.

CHAPTER 27
WARM UP THOSE VOCALS

Recently I ran a career confidence session at ITN in London. One of the women there told me she went for two job interviews and before the first one she hadn't spoken to anyone that morning. She fretted and fretted all morning, having not slept. When she got there, the first words out of her mouth that day were...

"Hello...cough, cough..."

She realised her throat and mouth had totally clammed up.

She realised she had not warmed up her vocal chords and she was 'rubbish'. She said the next day her interview was the total opposite. She had been out and about chatting and getting advice about what to say all morning, so she was motivated, lively and raring to go.

She got the job.

It's very simple to warm up your vocal chords. I have several opera-singing friends and they have many great warm up exercises. Here's one you can easily adopt...

Repeat after me.

She sells sea shells on the sea shore.

Now repeat it slowly.

She sells sea shells on the sea shore.

And repeat it again a tiny bit faster.

She sells sea shells on the sea shore.

Now faster!

She sells sea shells on the sea shore.

LOL – you're good. And faster still.

She sells sea shells on the sea shore.

Excellent. Well done!

With a tiny little screwed-up mouth – go on - smaller...

She sells sea shells on the sea shore.

SLOW
FASTER
SMALLER

TINY
TIP

**Other tongue twisters are available
and they DO WORK!**

Peter Piper picked a pickled pepper

Irish wrist watch – over and over

Red lorry yellow lorry

Red leather yellow leather

Have a go!

NOW PAUSE

To have a super lively tongue – yes tongue! Ewwww, you need to warm it up.

My old university drama teacher, David Bell, was a flamboyant man and brilliant vocal coach who was obsessed with *"your tongue darling, your tongue is a muscle; it needs to be worked."*

He once told me, *"You have a lazy tongue today"*.

Your tongue is a muscle and you need to flex and stretch it to warm up your voice. Weird but true!

So, to warm up your tongue, move it around inside your mouth – all over your mouth, round your teeth, top, bottom, roof, and the back all over. Feels strange, but it's warming up one of your essential speaking instruments.

Another few easy-peasy vocal exercises...

Humming (according to my opera singer pal).

Breathe slowly – in through the nose... and out through the mouth.

When you breathe in, hold for a moment, then hummmmm on your way out.

Now hummmm and make your lips vibrate.

Now do the same, but give me a high note!

VOCAL WARM–UP – DONE!

AND WET YOUR WHISTLE!

Remember – drink water so your mouth doesn't go dry.

Do not underestimate the power of your voice.

Keep your tongue, throat and saliva levels in check.

You will immediately look, sound and FEEL like a confident speaker.

and combat your Glossophobia by feeling vocally in control.

Speech – sorted!

TOFFEE
TIP

**Pretend to chew a massive
piece of toffee to warm up
your mouth**

**Inspired by David Bell, my old
drama teacher!**

CHAPTER 28
BRING OUT YOUR OOMPH!!

I had to keep energy levels UP at all times when I worked as a broadcasting producer for the BBC.

So my rule of oomph – or 'energy levels' – has always been a priority when it comes to communicating.

When you speak you NEED energy – it can make your delivery twice as good!

I'm so passionate about OOMPH and energy levels that I've gathered words that mean 'oomph' from all around the world...

I remember doing a masterclass in the House of Commons in Westminster for DFID (The Department for International Development). We had 12 locations from all over the world dialling in via WebEx – they texted in their words of oomph.

ENERGÍA — SPANISH
VAMOS —SPANISH
CHUTZPAH — YIDDISH
LET'S GO! — US
GIVE IT SOME WELLY! — UK
(YIA YOU) CHINESE FOR "ADD FUEL"
AUF GEHT'S — GERMAN
Поехали — POYEKHALI — RUSSIAN
ALLEZ — FRENCH
ELA "COME ON" IN GREEK
YOSHA! — JAPANESE
NISHATI! — SWAHILI

GET CRACKING

Try saying some of these fantastic upbeat
energising words – it makes you smile
and lifts you up!

I LOVE IT.

The best thing you can do before you attempt
to speak in public is wiggle your hips – put your
arms above you head and chant your favourite
OOMPH words – Jambo!

Oh yes, you feel good, don't you?

CHAPTER 29
EYES AND TEETH!

SMILE

And last but not least – this is the one thing that will help your Glossophobia more than ANYTHING!!

Eyes and teeth! Yes, that's right – SMILE!

OK – this is the easiest tip of all and probably the most effective when it comes to you looking, sounding and feeling confident when you speak.

Seriously – eyes and teeth!

OK – this tip reminds you to give good eye contact.

Eye contact is a MUST.

Putting your attention out onto others will help you feel more connected and social.

My good friend, the Harley Street therapist Olivia James, suggests while you are waiting to go on stage, make eye contact with a few people and smile at them. This helps to get your nervous system into social engagement and out of fight or flight mode. Then you should be able to deliver your talk without looking like a rabbit in the headlights and actually enjoy it.

Smile, smile, smile and you'll overcome Glossophobia a little bit more.

Here's why...

When you smile – your brain thinks you are happy. Pretty simple.

Your brain responds very quickly and simply to physical cues – like the power pose.

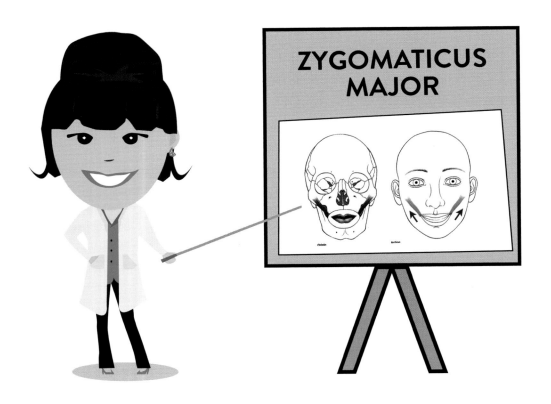

Here's the science bit – consider the Zygomatic major – that nerve that runs from the corners of your mouth to below your cheek bone.

Your brain thinks, *"oh look my Zygomatic major is turning upwards."*

Brain says, *"I must be happy!"*

Get Ziggy With it!

Have you heard of a smile experiment from the 1980s where a group of people were asked to hold a pencil between their teeth?

Try it...

The pencil forced them to smile – their zygomatic major would turn upwards.

Another group were asked to hold a pencil with their lips so their mouths were turned downwards.

The groups were shown videos and the people with the upturned smiles made more positive comments than the group with the downward mouth.

Hence – when your zygomatic major is turned upwards – your brain thinks positive, happy thoughts.

One of my clients told me her entire office tried this experiment for a whole morning and it really did work. But all the pencils got ruined because of the bite marks!

So, when I used to say in the live TV studio at the BBC:

"Eyes and teeth!"

Yes, the audience got a better reaction.

There's more to that comment than meets the eye!

In a nutshell – the ultimate speaking hack – eyes and teeth! Smile.

TOOTHY TIP!

Give good eye contact to your audience!
Putting your attention out onto others will help you feel more connected and social. It will get you out of fight-or-flight mode.

Olivia James - Harley Street performance and confidence therapist

CHAPTER 30
AND FINALLY —
THIS COULD BE YOU!

Elaine & Esther in Shoreditch , London

"THREE LITTLE WORDS THAT CHANGED MY LIFE"

By Dr Elaine Heslop, Director, Lucidity Services Ltd

On a rainy Tuesday I joined a conference call and was asked to "tell my story" at the firm's annual partner conference in 2015. The brief: a 10-minute slot right after the morning keynote. Daunted, I said "yes", and the fear set in.

A few weeks later I found myself at the back of a hotel ballroom, sitting next to the sound engineers, hoping that the floor would swallow me up. I watched and listened to the speaker before me: a 19-year-old YouTube sensation who was mesmerising...

NASA had named an asteroid after him!

He was actually a rocket scientist!

...And I was just me. The member of staff they'd invited along to speak about the business that I'd founded – presumably to keep it real. How was I going to follow this?

As my catatonic state deepened, a heart-warming video began to play...

He'd been a praise singer for Nelson Mandela!

He knew the Obamas, Bill Gates, Mark Zuckerberg!

...and now he had a standing ovation...

As the entire room rose to its feet, I had two options: leave via the door to my left or go on and deploy every single piece of advice I had been given. Walking slowly to the edge of the stage, I stopped and smiled at the room, I thrust out my arms...

"Wasn't that fantastic!"...

In three little words I brought the energy from his speech into mine, and I told my story. It went well. I did it! Four years later I still bump into people who ask me "How did you do that?"

The answer, simply, was Esther.

In the weeks that had passed between the invite and conference day, Esther put me through my paces. The enclosed glass room in my employer's basement had a fishbowl quality that mirrored how I felt: exposed. Her ability to bring to bear her expertise as a BBC producer was transformational. Her "eyes and teeth" mantra, focus on my audience, and life-saving tips on following a standing ovation helped me to make the speech of my life. Public speaking and networking are things many people find difficult. In my experience, Esther quickly gets the measure of her clients. She's empathetic but doesn't pull her punches. She builds confidence by sharing her expertise with humour, and giving honest feedback. She's brilliant!

WELL, THANK YOU ELAINE, YOU ARE BRILLIANT TOO!

THANK YOU.

THANK YOU FOR READING THIS.
THANK YOU FOR TAKING THIS STEP.
YOU WILL OVERCOME YOUR GLOSSOPHOBIA.
GO ON, GET OUT THERE, YOU'LL BE AWESOME.

EYES AND TEETH!

ACKNOWLEDGEMENTS

THANK YOU...

for inspiring me to write this book.

A special thank you to the fantastic Kim Duke, my coach, friend and mentor who told me not so long ago to "write" when I thought I couldn't.

"If you can speak you can write... write what you think is rubbish and let me edit you."

She gave me the courage to step outside my comfort zone.

Thanks to Patrick, Laurence and the team at LMPP design. I cannot thank you enough for your creativity and flashes of inspiration.

Thanks to Filament Publishing for holding my hand when it all looked too overwhelming.

Thanks to Adam, my daughter Mirabelle and son Truman for understanding.

Thank you, Richard, Hayley and Rozi from A Thousand Monkeys, for your wise & wonderful words & helping with my blurbaphobia!

Gemma Guise, you're a PR genius. Claire Langmend you are the best you've - been my rock. Cathy Wilcox, you are a grammatical lifesaver.

If you are worried and anxious about stepping into the spotlight, don't beat yourself up. This will help you. Enjoy.

LET'S CONNECT

If you want more tips, blogs and my fun video tips do go to my website.

You'll love it.

Website: **www.estherstanhope.com**

LinkedIn: **Please connect with me**

Email: **impact@estherstanhope.com**

Twitter: **@EstherStanhope1**

Facebook: **EstherStanhopeImpactGuru**

NOTES

NOTES

NOTES

NOTES

NOTES

NOTES

NOTES

NOTES